Welcome

When the winter chills sweep in and we start to batten down the hatches, it's all too easy to go into hibernation mode and watch the clocks ticking away in anticipation of warmer days. However, there's so much joy to be found by staying at home during the colder period. In this brand-new title, we'll show you how to turn your home into a winter haven, from how to illuminate darker evenings with a roaring fire in your fireplace, to tips on creating a secluded nook to snuggle into in the evenings. We'll also share our favourite crafts to help pass the time and up the snug factor in your home, and winter warmer recipes to keep you and your kitchen toasty. Elsewhere, we'll share practical advice on keeping your home protected against inclement weather, including how to bleed radiators and over-winter your tools, and how to use your time wisely to declutter.

The content in this book is aimed at providing inspiration for furniture, decorating, and storage solutions that can work in your home. Specific products are referenced within the book as a guide only – while the trends, prices and availability of products was correct at the time of original publication, please be aware this information is subject to change.

Contents

06
MAINTAIN YOUR HOME OVER WINTER
These household tasks and home improvement ideas will brighten up your winter

16
HOME COMFORTS
Take inspiration from the changing seasons to create cosy, protective spaces that are perfect for hibernating

22
10 WAYS TO COSY UP A BEDROOM
Swapping that warm spot on the sofa for a chilly bedroom can be a shock, so create all the warm feels with these ideas

27
WARM TOUCH
Transform an old jumper into a beautiful hot water bottle cover, perfect for staving off seasonal chills

28
LOVE YOUR LARDER
It's harvest time, so take the opportunity to check food stores, tidy shelves and restock for the new season

32
FIRESIDE SUPPERS
We're looking forward to colder nights and coming home to crowd-pleasing one pots

38
NOSTALGIC CHOCOLATE PUDS
Go retro with our old-school favourites

42
HOW TO GET RID OF EMOTIONAL CLUTTER
Winter is a great time to do a clear out, but are you finding it hard to let go? Our experts advise…

46
TIDY UP TIME
The secret to a beautiful home is plenty of storage to hide away clutter, so find a place for everything with our round-up of the best solutions

51
WARMING DRINKS
Stay toasty this winter with five creative hot drinks that you can make it home

52
RUSTIC RETREAT
Create cabin-inspired spaces by decorating with natural materials, earthy, tones, and organic textures

60
FILL YOUR HOME WITH BOOKS
Literature lover? A home library, or reading nook could be the escape from everyday life that you've been waiting for…

63
BOOK KEEP
Sew this quick-stitch bookmark so you won't lose your place

64
RECHARGING AT HOME
Enthusiasm for having your own at-home retreat is on the rise, from garden cabins to spa bathrooms. But why do we need that emotional escape room?

68
COSY CORNER
These simple designs steps are all you need to ensure your reading nook (or box-set bolthole) is the serene spot you're after

71
ALL ABLAZE
Create a natural alternative to shop-bought firelighters and fill your home with beautiful seasonal scents

72
BURNING BRIGHT
What are you looking for a decorative traditional fireplace or a cosy and cost-effective stove, these designs create the perfect antidote to cold autumn evenings

76
QUICK-FIX REFRESH
A flick of paint in a flash of colour – spend an hour or two this winter to create these in-the-moment makeovers for your space

22

52

72

104

80
HOMESPUN HIGHLANDS
Bring heartwarming comfort to winter interiors, with wool blankets, tactile quilts and handmade pieces inspired by Scottish bothies and rural retreats

86
BOOT ROOM
These simple design ingredients are all you need to create a practical dedicated space for your shoes and outdoor gear

89
RUSTIC GLOW
Banish the dark nights with these simple, yet atmospheric potted candle holders

90
PULL UP YOUR BOOTS
Keep your home organised during the festive chaos by making sure that wet coats and muddy shoes have a home in a practical, but also pretty space

95
WINTERY ONE-POTS
Nourishing dishes filled with comforting flavours – ideal for cosy weekends at home

100
COSY PUDDINGS
A lighter take on some of your favourite desserts

104
WINTER AL FRESCO
Get cosy outdoors with these simple updates and turn your garden into a cocooning, entertaining space to celebrate with family and friends

110
A WINTER'S TALE
There's cold comfort to be had in the winter garden as the seasons, most resilient plants reveal their true beauty

116
I SPY... IN MY WINTER GARDEN
Doctor Sarah Spinney reveals what to look out for

117
FEED THE BIRDS
Keep feathered friends well-fed over winter by creating this festive swag with a difference

118
FREEZE FRAME
Capture the beauty of your garden and the countryside in winter with our expert photography guide

122
BATHING BEAUTY
Embrace the relaxing qualities of lavender with this soap recipe that combines soothing essential oils and dried flower buds

123
WARMING UP
Whether you choose to build your own, or buy a ready-made design, enjoy evenings in the garden, even as the mercury drops with a cosy fire pit

126
NEW YEAR'S RESOLUTIONS
Look forward to a fresh start and commit to improving your home and garden, learning new skills, and making a positive impact with these ideas

Winter Home 05

Maintain your home over winter

These household tasks and home improvement ideas will brighten up your winter

Home becomes an even bigger part of our world during winter. As the weather gets colder and the nights grow longer, we spend more of our time indoors – 75% of our waking hours, according to one recent survey. For many people, including many homemakers, children, retirees and remote workers, much of that indoor time is home-based.

To make these days as pleasant and comfortable as possible, we need to pay attention to our homes, as well as the appliances and systems that make them tick. From heating maintenance and insulation upgrades to planning for transformative long-term projects, there's a wealth of opportunities for better living within these four walls.

Winterise your appliances and tools

Before you plan any new projects to improve your home this winter, take the time to protect what you've got. Certain parts of the building, as well as some of your appliances and possessions, will need extra maintenance to prepare them for different usage patterns or conditions during winter. There's a great word for this process that's popular in North America: winterisation.

HEATING APPLIANCES

What better way to start winterising your home than by giving some TLC to your heating appliances? Many of these warmth-givers – from radiators and boilers to solid fuel stoves – will have been used rarely, or not at all, since the spring.

If you've noticed a fusty smell the first time a radiator is heated up in the winter, the likely culprit is a buildup of dust or dirt. These particles accumulate over spring and summer, and you can smell them burning off as the radiator heats up. It's hardly ideal for your indoor air quality, and potentially aggravating for those with allergies.

Cleaning your radiators before you start using the central heating will deal with some of the dust before it can be incinerated. If the radiators have removable panels on the sides and top (and you're confident that you'll be able to reattach them), pop these off to gain better access.

You can then start cleaning using a long duster, or hoovering up easy-to-reach dust using a vacuum cleaner with a furniture brush attachment. For stubborn dirt, wipe surfaces first with a damp cloth, and then with a dry cloth to make sure the radiator is not left wet.

To ensure efficient heating, you should also bleed your radiators. This simply means

HOW TO BLEED A RADIATOR

It's a simple task, but one that many of us overlook in the colder months. Ensuring that your heating is working as it should will help you to keep your home toasty and your energy bills low.

1. Make sure the heating system is turned off and the radiator is cool.

2. Identify the bleed valve, located at one of the top corners of the radiator.

3. Place a towel and bowl underneath the bleed valve.

4. Slowly loosen the bleed valve using a radiator key or flat-head screwdriver (depending on the type of valve), until you hear air escaping.

5. When water starts coming out of the valve, tighten the valve back up again.

Winter Home 07

releasing any trapped air which may have accumulated inside the radiator, reducing its ability to fill with hot water and heat the space effectively.

Households with a solid fuel stove will be looking forward to some homely fires as the nights draw in. Fuels such as seasoned firewood logs and biomass briquettes are usually at their most expensive during the winter heating season, so you could save money by stocking up a little earlier in the year. Make sure you choose a fuel that's compatible with your stove, and store it off the ground in a dry, well-ventilated place.

But before you throw your kindling onto the grate, consider the condition of your chimney – especially the flue lining, which is the flexible piping that channels fumes up from the stove and out through the chimney stack. The buildup of soot or creosote within this pipe carries serious dangers, including chimney fires (over 3,000 occur in the UK each year) and re-entry of dangerous gases into the room.

HETAS, the national authority on domestic solid fuel heating, recommends getting your chimney swept regularly to manage these risks. Twice per year is the recommended frequency if you're burning wood, while once per year is considered sufficient for households using smokeless fuels. The best timing for the job is either just before the winter heating season or straight after it.

If you have a combi boiler, you'll need to get it serviced annually by a Gas Safe accredited technician, in order to ensure its safe operation and keep its warranty valid. We would recommend getting this done before the coldest winter weather arrives (unless you've already dealt with it during the summer or autumn months).

The technician might find issues with the boiler which necessitate a temporary shut-off for repairs, or even replacement. It's best to reserve this possibility for milder months, when you'd be more comfortable without central heating. Boiler repairs and replacements can take anywhere from a few hours to several days.

Underfloor heating (UFH) does not usually require much maintenance. However, some households choose to get their UFH serviced annually. Autumn or early winter would be a smart time to get this done, allowing for issues to be identified and fixed before the weather gets uncomfortably cold.

Heat pumps are becoming more popular in UK homes, and if you have one of these energy-efficient systems, this will be another item for your maintenance checklist. In addition to the annual servicing generally required for both air-source heat pumps (ASHPs) and ground-source heat pumps

WINTERISE A GAS-FUELLED POWER TOOL

Winterisation has a special meaning for gas-powered tools. If you own a petrol-powered tool, follow these steps:

1. Identify the fuel tank on your gas-powered tool.

2. Either drain the fuel or add a liquid stabiliser product to the partially filled tank. Stabiliser prevents the fuel from degrading, which could cause clogging, corrosion and other issues.

3. If the tool has an oil tank, make sure this is filled completely with fresh oil.

4. Consider changing the spark plug. It's generally advised to do this at least once per year.

5. Clean the engine filters (or replace them if they're in poor condition).

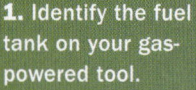

(GSHPs), ASHPs often require extra attention during autumn and winter, as their above-ground air inputs are prone to blockage by fallen leaves and other debris. These must be cleared out to preserve the system's airflow and efficient performance.

GARDEN AND DIY TOOLS

Winter is downtime for many of your garden and DIY tools. You might still need your cordless drill for easy jobs around the house, but you probably won't get as much use out of tools like circular saws, which are often used outdoors to prevent dust pollution inside the home. And of course, there'll be little use for your hedge trimmer or lawnmower while there's limited growth in the garden.

Now is the time to maintain and winterise these items, so that you can take them out of storage in good condition when spring comes back around.

For most tools, the main requirements are to ensure the item is clean, dry and safely stored. Give each tool a thorough wipe to remove debris from the materials or plants you've used it on. In some cases, you'll need to use a stiff brush (or even methylated spirits, while wearing good PPE) to remove the most stubborn dirt and grime. Failure to clean tools before winter storage can lead to rusting, blockages and impaired function.

Always dry tools very thoroughly after cleaning, especially if you've used water or another liquid to lift away dirt (where allowed by the manufacturer's instructions). You might also need to oil parts that rub against each other, such as the blades on a pair of secateurs. A general-purpose oil such as '3-IN-ONE' will usually do the trick.

Storing tools properly is also crucial to their good condition through the seasons. If they're kept in an outbuilding such as a garden shed, keep them raised off the ground on shelves, racking, or even a makeshift platform such as a wooden pallet. Make sure they're sheltered from the winter weather, and keep them inside a container such as a hard case or the original box.

If you have some cordless tools, then you'll also need to take good care of the lithium-ion batteries needed to power them. Due to the gradual deterioration of internal components such as electrodes, every lithium-ion battery will eventually stop working. Their lifespans range significantly, from just a few years to a decade or more. A key factor in determining the length of effective functioning – along with the quality of a battery and how much you use it – is how you store it over winter.

Good battery maintenance habits will help this essential accessory to work well for a longer period. Lithium-ion batteries deteriorate more quickly when they are left with either a high or low level of charge, due to the strain these states place upon certain battery components. Most manufacturers recommend charging these batteries to around 40-60% before storage, in order to minimise their deterioration.

Of course, you should also make sure your lithium-ion batteries are stored in a dry place to prevent rusting or water damage. Most are designed to be kept at household temperatures, so it might be worth bringing your batteries in from the shed over winter.

Weather-proof your home for a cosy winter

There's plenty we can do to make our homes warmer – and make a difference to our energy use and utility bills – before the weather turns. One possibility is adding insulation to poorly insulated spaces.

For many homeowners, the most accessible type to improve is loft insulation. Even if your loft already has insulation, it might not meet the latest energy efficiency standards. The relevant building regulation, 'Approved Document L', stipulates that the insulation used in this space should be at least 270mm thick (if using mineral wool, which is now often preferred to fibreglass). Recent surveys reveal that many UK homes have far thinner loft insulation, with 33% shown to have an insulative layer measuring less than 125mm – or none at all.

If your loft has safe access and you feel confident about going into the space using a suitable ladder, go and assess the insulation currently in place. Is it deep enough, and is it well distributed throughout the loft so that the room below is fully insulated? Remember that some forms of insulation, such as fibreglass, are unsafe to breathe. Wear a good mask, safety goggles and gloves while handling the old material.

You may find that the loft insulation could be thickened or distributed more widely in certain places. If you are a confident DIYer, you might be able to add new insulation where it's needed, buying the material from a hardware retailer, cutting it to size using a craft knife, and then rolling it out inside the loft to cover the required areas. Never put your weight on any part of the loft that might not be able to support you – or else you may end up with your leg dangling down through the bedroom ceiling.

Perhaps with the risks of loft-based DIY in mind, some homeowners choose to get this job done by a professional. This typically adds a labour cost of around £250 per day, and many loft insulation fittings can be completed within a few days or less.

Insulating the walls of a building is a far costlier and more disruptive project that's typically undertaken as part of a full-blown home renovation. Few homeowners would be happy to take this on as a DIY project, and according to Checkatrade, the costs of getting external wall insulation professionally installed can range from around £6,000 to £30,000, depending on factors including the size of the property.

The installation of wall insulation is generally best reserved for milder times of year, but if your home is not insulated (a common issue with Edwardian or older

HOW TO INSULATE A LOFT HATCH

You might have already insulated your loft, but have you ever thought about doing the same for your loft hatch? This feature can create a significant cold spot in the home, allowing heat from the living space below to escape into the loft. If your loft hatch is not insulated, it's probably making your home cooler and increasing your heating bills. The good news is that you can fix this quickly and cheaply, using minimal tools and materials.

1. Gather your materials. You'll need a craft knife, some non-solvent grab adhesive, a small section of polyurethane insulation and a tape measure.

2. Measure the loft hatch panel. (Measure twice, cut once!)

3. Cut the polyurethane insulation to size. You can do this using your craft knife or a good pair of shears.

4. Glue the polyurethane panel to the upper side of your loft hatch. Your loft hatch is now insulated!

This is a quick and easy project, but it does involve working at height. Before starting work, make sure that you take proper precautions such as wearing appropriate PPE and using a good, reliable ladder to access the loft.

Maintain your home over winter

properties), then it's worth considering. A research team led by the Leeds Sustainability Institute (LSI) at Leeds Beckett University has found that adding solid wall insulation can decrease the energy use of a property that previously had poor energy performance by as much as 30%.

As we all know, British winters are wet as well as chilly. Whether you're in Glasgow, London, Cardiff or Belfast, rainfall tends to peak between October and January.

Dealing with rain, humidity, damp and related problems such as mould and mildew often rises to the tops of our to-do lists at this time of year – and thankfully, there are plenty of things we can do to safeguard our homes against the wet.

Why not start in the gutter? Rainwater runs into these troughs from all sides of the roofing, then travels into the drainpipe and under the ground. You probably won't give this much thought when your guttering is working correctly, but a blocked gutter may soon demand your attention. In some cases, the water trapped or diverted by a blocked gutter can cause damage to brickwork and roofing, or encourage the development of mould.

Gutters are most commonly blocked during autumn and winter, when fallen leaves tend to accumulate (although there are other potential blockages such as mosses and deceased animals). The best solution is to get your guttering cleaned. This can cost anywhere from around £50 to £100s, with prices varying based on the length of guttering, access requirements and other factors.

Another common cause of winter damp and mould is humidity. While the outdoor air tends to be relatively dry at this time of year, our lifestyle can cause the air inside our homes to become very humid during the colder months. When you are doing things like drying wet laundry indoors and you're rarely leaving windows open, moisture has nowhere to go but into the air and onto your surfaces and belongings.

Extraction is one way to deal with some of the moisture from daily living. Installing an extractor fan in the bathroom and a vented kitchen extractor will reduce the added humidity, directing vapour and steam straight from two of their most significant sources to the outer air.

You might also consider running a dehumidifier. These appliances draw in air and pass it over cooling components, which cause water vapour to condense and fall into a receptacle before the air (now with a reduced water content) is passed back into the room.

Properties with unmanageable damp problems may require a more robust solution, such as damp coursing. This major structural project involves the addition of waterproof layers into walls and/or flooring. It's a job to get done during warmer weather – and only if you really need it.

Planning for the year ahead

Winter weather often draws attention to a building's structural issues (or causes new ones). You might notice that the roof is leaking, rain is coming down the chimney, or that it's time to replace draughty or condensation-coated glazing. Or perhaps an abundance of festive visitors will confirm what you've long expected: that you could use a little more living space.

Some of these cases should be addressed as quickly as possible. For instance, caulking around a draughty window or applying self-adhesive draught strips can reduce the ingress of cold air, at least in the short term.

However, it's often best to plan for major structural works over the winter, then tackle them during finer weather in spring or summer. The biggest projects often involve opening a section of the building to the elements, and this is best avoided while rain, cold, wind or even snow could delay work or damage the home's interior.

Maintain your home over winter

HOW TO PLAN MAJOR STRUCTURAL CHANGES TO YOUR HOME

You might not be able to get spades in the ground this winter – perhaps literally – but there's no better time to do the hard, satisfying mental work of planning. The particulars will vary from one project to another, but you'll usually need to work through the following planning phases:

Planning permission. Some major structural changes require planning permission – especially if the work will extend your home or significantly alter its external appearance. To find out whether your project requires planning permission, you'll need to consult with your Local Planning Authority (LPA), via the local authority. Listed buildings and homes located in conservation areas are generally subject to stricter planning requirements.

Budgeting. Before you start spending money on formalising your home improvement plans, it pays to establish whether the project will be affordable. We'd recommend obtaining quotes from multiple local contractors and materials suppliers to work out a realistic estimate. Bear in mind that the costs of labour and materials have risen considerably in recent years, and these trends may continue.

Design. Some home improvements require a significant design process. If you're going to extend the property, you would be well advised to commission an architect to create drawings for the extension. This is not a legal requirement, but architect's drawings are a valuable asset in the planning permission process. Typically, an architect's expertise will also help to ensure your extension is safely designed, liveable and attractive.

We'd recommend planning, rather than completing, projects such as the following during winter:

Re-roofing: While partial roof repairs might be unavoidable in the winter, fully re-roofing a building is best done during spring or later.

Extending the property: The new extension of your home will be vulnerable to wind, rain and cold throughout much of the building process. At some stages, existing rooms might also be open to the elements.

Constructing outbuildings: Structures like sunrooms and sheds will also be open to the elements during assembly.

Traditional repointing: The traditional lime mortar used in a heritage repointing project needs plenty of time and fine weather so that it can set successfully.

If you're keen to get on with some DIY this winter, there are plenty of options that won't expose your home or materials to the harsh weather – not too much, at least.

Think about fixtures: the various items which can be fixed to the internal walls of your home. Shelves, curtain rails, wall-mounted appliances, mirrors and various other life-enhancing additions can all be put up without the need for outdoor work (perhaps with the exception of homemade wooden shelves, which may need to be cut to size outside).

Plumbing tasks are often winter-appropriate, too. If you need to fix a leaky tap, fit a new shower head or even install a new sink basin, now would be an excellent time to get the job done, while other DIY projects await the warmer weather that'll be here before we know it.

To get the best out of winter, we need to winterise our thinking, as well as our homes. As we narrow our focus to suit the season, we may realise just how much potential exists – and how much more there is to do – right before our eyes.

Home comforts

As summer fades and autumn closes in, take inspiration from the changing seasons to create cosy, protective spaces that are perfect for hibernating. Sitting grounding neutrals and evergreens alongside earthy textures and natural prints will guarantee enduring charm

WINDING DOWN
As the nights draw in and the fireside beckons, prepare your sitting room for autumn living by introducing plenty of snug seating and tactile fabrics and throws. Covered in cosy fleece, The White Company's Sheepskin chair is ideal for hunkering down, while its Pearl sheepskin round pouffe, and Pearl curly sheepskin stool make welcome rests for weary legs after country walks.

Home comforts

IT'S THE LITTLE THINGS
Foraged hedgerow treasures make for beautiful autumnal displays, so be sure to take a closer look as you venture out on your autumn walks. Sculptural seed pods and fallen leaves will look beautiful hung from branches in Rowen & Wren's bud vases.

EMBRACE NATURE
Bring seasonal charm and colour to neutral spaces with autumnal-themed artwork. Based on an original watercolour, this Pheasant and Deer wall hanging, from Sam Wilson Studio, really shines when set against a moody charcoal wall.

AUTUMN PALETTE
From rich orange to myriad earthy greens, let the colours of nature's harvest inspire a cosy room scheme. Ornamental squashes are brilliant for adding seasonal style, too. Display on windowsills or mantelpieces, or grouped on a dish to as a centrepiece for a relaxed dinner table laid with linen from Rowen & Wren.

SITTING PRETTY
To bring a hint of pattern to a soothing scheme, consider covering an armchair in a fabric from Sanderson's A Celebration of the National Trust Collection, which draws on the beauty of the British countryside. A chinoiserie-inspired design set on an atmospheric navy, this Lophura print is effortlessly elegant.

RUSTIC CHARM
As the heart of the home, the kitchen is where we spend most of our time, so making it welcoming and calm is essential. For timeless appeal, let rustic period features take the lead, such as weathered beams and flagstone floors, while opting for base cabinets only will help keep the space feeling open and airy. Inextricably linked with the soothing and enduring beauty of nature, green is a brilliant colour for everyday spaces like kitchens. Plain English's Army Camp shade, pictured here on its bespoke cabinetry really grounds this space and beautifully complements natural wood and stone.

TALES FROM THE ORCHARD
Cosy corners papered in whimsical natural prints make perfect escapes when the weather starts to turn. Based on a handpainted design that celebrates the seasonal changes of an apple tree, from blossom to ripening fruit, this Ingrid Marie paper from Boråstapeter will rekindle magical memories of summer in the countryside. From Wallpaper Direct, it's available in moody teal for a cocooning feel, or an uplifting neutral.

Clockwise from top left: Under Hillway Coppice linen in Ruby, Susie Hetherington; Quantock QUAN-012 linen, Fermoie; Zanzibar linen in Tobacco/Raspberry, Penny Morrison; Heathland linen, Sam Wilson Studio

SLEEPING BEAUTY

With long nights on the horizon, now is the time to make sure the bedroom is a restful and cosy space. Offering a varied patina and a subtle spectrum of warm neutral tones, distressed plaster walls would make a soothing backdrop. Why not mimic the texture on the floor using a woven rug such as this Yaro extra-large woven hemp rug, from Graham & Green? Pared-back versions of French-style designs, Graham & Green's Alva king-size bed and side table are perfect for bringing subtle elegance to a quiet space. Finish the look with Graham & Green's Downton wall sconces, and cushions in an array of artisan linens in autumnal colours.

Home comforts

SOFT TOUCH
No bedroom is complete without plenty of cushions and throws for snuggling down on crisp winter mornings. If you love the layered vintage look, Projektityyny has plenty of embroidered blankets, patchwork quilts, and ruffle trim cushions in checks, stripes and florals ready for mixing and matching.

MOODY BOTANICALS
As the seasons turn, don't be afraid to embrace nature's darker side. Flower and leaf prints set against teals, charcoals and black will bring whimsy while giving rooms atmosphere and a quirky twist; we love this Flora design from Boråstapeter. If wall-to-wall is too much, try a small project like papering a tray.

INTO THE ARBORETUM
Immerse yourself in the magic of an autumn woodland with Cole & Son's Martyn Lawrence Bullard Royal Fernery wallpaper covered in abundant leaf forms in myriad greens. To temper the rich tapestry print, pair with the clean lines of Ikea's Hemnes bed frame, Kornsjö side table, and plain linen bedding.

COSY CORNERS
Lighting plays an essential role in creating the perfect reading nook. Combining a good mix of ambient and task lighting will ensure a cosy atmosphere while providing practical light to read by. From its Oxford bronze wall lights to its Pimlico floor lamp, David Hunt Lighting has plenty of classic designs to choose from.

1 USE NATURAL FIBRES

One of the best ways to retain heat is to use temperature-regulating materials for your bed. 'Rather than leaving your heating on overnight, choose a natural mattress filling that will help keep you warm and regulate your temperature,' advises Adam Black, co-founder of Button & Sprung. The same goes for your duvet and pillow fillings. 'As soon as you get into bed,' says Adam, 'natural fillings such as wool respond to your body's warmth, to keep you at a comfortable temperature. No external heating required.'

Bedding and throws in natural materials such as wool are excellent at regulating your body temperature while you sleep

10 ways to cosy up a bedroom

Swapping that warm spot on the sofa for a chilly bedroom can be a shock, so create all the warm feels with these ideas

A gorgeous view but try to minimise the draughts – particularly around older windows

10 ways to cosy up a bedroom

2 BLOCK DRAUGHTS

It can be a fiddly job, but spending a little time draught-proofing will make your bedroom cosier. 'Put draught excluders at the bottom of doors and around the seals of windows. You can even get inflatable ones for chimneys,' says Stephen Hankinson, energy expert at Electric Radiators Direct. 'They cost very little and are an effective way of ensuring you're not losing heat.' Options include screw-on door brush strips, self-adhesive tapes and foam strips. But be careful not to block window vents, as these are needed to prevent damp and mould developing.

3 SHUT THE DOOR

This is going to be a contentious idea for those whose lives revolve around a four-legged friend who likes to come and go during the night! However, a lot of heat is lost simply by leaving the doors open around the house. 'It's one of the easiest ways to lose heat in your home,' explains Jess Steele, heating technology expert at Best Heating. 'Pre-heating is wasted and a cosy room becomes cold within a matter of minutes when the door is left open. Keep the door shut to trap the heat in the room, maintaining its warmth for longer.'

In a room this size it's important to keep the doors closed to prevent heat escaping

4 SIZE UP BEDDING

Buying a duvet that's a size larger than your bed frame can help give you a warmer night's sleep too. This is especially true if you find yourself rolling to the edge of the bed with your feet or hands poking out into the cold air beyond. 'I always recommend choosing a duvet one size larger than the bed frame so that it drapes over the edges of the bed, softening the look of the whole room while offering plenty of warmth,' explains Georgia Metcalfe, founder and creative director of French Bedroom. 'A larger duvet will also feel heavier, creating a sense of security and helping towards a great night's sleep.'

Add a luxurious look to your sleep space with a duvet that drapes over the sides of the bed, as well as layers of cosy throws to keep you warm

5 WARM THE BED

Slipping between chilly sheets can make the bed feel colder than it is. Used safely, a good old-fashioned hot water bottle is an easy way to warm it up first. Don't be tempted to use a wheat bag – fire safety officers now warn against them because they continue to heat up after being microwaved and can set bedding alight. Gareth Kloet, energy spokesperson at Go.Compare, suggests, 'An electric blanket is another great option for keeping warm and could cost less than you think at an estimated 4p an hour*.' Plus it will only need to be switched on for a short time before you turn in. Hop into an already warmed bed on a chilly night and you'll be in the land of nod in no time.

6 CHECK YOUR DUVET

How old is yours? The Sleep Council recommends that we replace a duvet after five years, although this will depend on its original quality. Obvious signs of age include fraying and holes, but look for places where the filling is flat because it can break down over time.

Consider the tog rating, too: 'A tog is essentially a measure of how well a duvet holds heat,' explains Lucy Ackroyd, head of design at Christy. 'Most cold sleepers will get sufficient warmth from a 13.5 tog duvet. If you tend to overheat at night, then go for a 10.5 tog duvet and add a blanket that you can easily remove if you need to.'

Make sure your duvet is up to scratch – a higher tog rating is a good idea if you are a chilly type

*BASED ON APPLIANCE WATTAGES LISTED BY CENTRE FOR SUSTAINABLE ENERGY. ENERGY PRICES BASED ON THE ENERGY PRICE CAP UNIT RATE OF 28P/KWH, NOT SPECIFIC TO YOUR HOUSEHOLD'S ENERGY TARIFF, USAGE OR REGION

With a large balcony window and skylight, a loft room like this needs good insulating curtains and blinds in the winter months

Rich dark hues create cosiness, but if this midnight shade is a step too far, earthy terracotta is warm and cossetting

7 WRAP WINDOWS

Bedrooms lose a lot of heat through the windows, so it's a cold spot to tackle when temperatures drop in autumn. Melissa Denham, interior design expert at Hammonds Furniture, advises, 'Swap out blinds or sheer, lightweight curtains for some that are made from a heavier material. Curtains made from materials such as wool or velvet, or (even better) curtains with a thermal lining, will stop your rooms losing heat, saving you money on your energy bills too.' Another option is to hang two pairs of curtains, or a blind plus curtains to keep in the heat.

8 BAN WHITE WALLS

'Making your home feel toasty is not just about the temperature,' explains Emma Bestley, co-founder of paint company Yes Colours. 'How you warm up your space visually has an impact on how you feel during the colder months, too.'

Nicolene Mausenbaum, director of Dezyna Interiors, recommends, 'Using earthy colours like terracotta on your walls will help create a warm, cosy atmosphere.' If you don't want to do a full room redo, updating bedding, curtains and accessories in warmer hues can have the same effect.

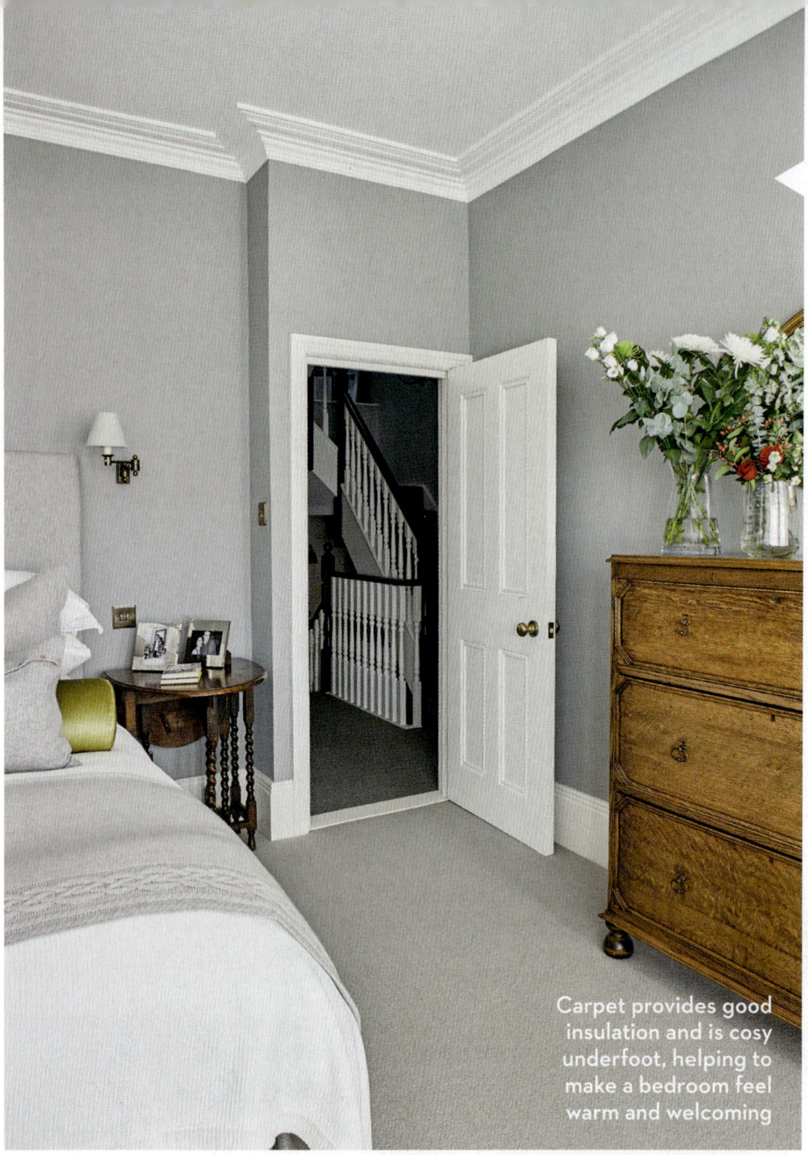

Carpet provides good insulation and is cosy underfoot, helping to make a bedroom feel warm and welcoming

9 FIT A CARPET

If you're considering replacing bedroom flooring, carpet could be the best option. 'Carpet is an excellent form of insulation as it increases your home's ability to retain warmth,' explain the experts at Tapi Carpets & Floors. 'The best flooring to help keep a home warm without turning on the heating is a high tog-rated carpet combined with the right underlay for that carpet type. Tog ratings are the best indicators of natural insulation; aim for a rating of 2.5 to 4 (including underlay).

10 LAY RUGS

While original floorboards or laminate flooring look great, they can be very cold underfoot, so it's a good idea to go rug shopping to complement them without completely covering them. 'When your floors are left uncovered, they can feel very cold,' says Matthew Jenkins, heating expert at MyJobQuote. 'This is especially true for stone or hardwood floors. You can lose a lot of your home's heat through this type of floor, so laying a rug can prevent some of the heat loss, as well as being softer and cosier to walk on.'

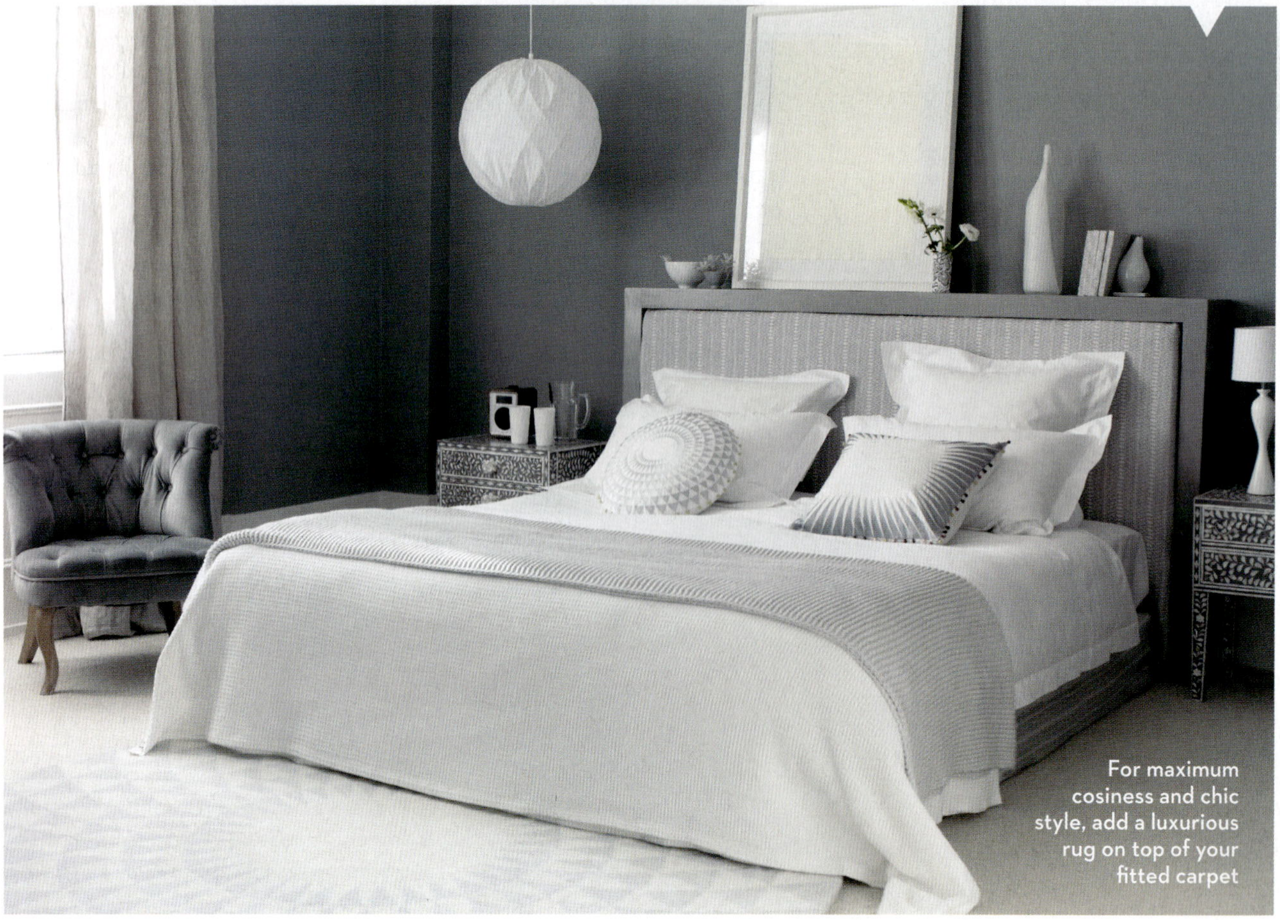

For maximum cosiness and chic style, add a luxurious rug on top of your fitted carpet

FEATURE AMY HODGE, VANESSA RICHMOND **PHOTOGRAPHS** FUTURECONTENTHUB.COM/JAMES FRENCH, JEREMY PHILLIPS, DOMINIC BLACKMORE, OLIVER GORDON, TIM YOUNG, COLIN POOLE, JOANNA HENDERSON, POLLY WREFORD

Warm touch

Transform an old jumper into a beautiful hot water bottle cover, perfect for staving off seasonal chills

Put away your knitting needles and turn your hand to some upcycling with this craft project that transforms an old jumper into a cosy hot water bottle cover. Surprisingly easy to create, it only takes an hour or two to craft, and would make a perfect gift for a loved one, too – especially if you follow our last step to personalise it.

YOU WILL NEED
● A hot water bottle ● An old turtleneck cable-knit jumper ● Tailor's chalk ● Fabric shears ● Pins ● Needle and thread ● Sewing machine (optional) ● Fabric glue (such as Bostik Sew Simple)

1. Search the back of your wardrobe or drawers for an old cable-knit turtleneck jumper that you no longer wear, or pick up a bargain at your local charity shop.
2. Wash and dry the jumper, then turn it inside out and lay it out on a flat surface. The back of the jumper will become the back of the hot water bottle cover, and the turtleneck will be the top.
3. Lay your hot water bottle on top of the jumper, with the neck of the bottle lined up with the jumper's turtleneck. Trace around it using tailor's chalk.
4. Remove the bottle and pin the back and the front together along what will be the seam. Hand sew or use a sewing machine to stitch the layers together, leaving the top of the turtleneck open, as this is how you will get the bottle in and out of the cover. Sew twice to guard against any unravelling.
5. Cut out the cover, approximately 1cm (3/8") from the seam and apply fabric glue on all the edges to stop them from unravelling. Turn right-side out and insert the hot water bottle through the turtleneck.
6. Personalise the cover by cutting out the initial or name of the person you are giving it to in felt or fabric, and appliqué it to the front. Using pretty, patterned material makes a nice contrast to the plain wool of the jumper.

Love your larder

It's harvest time, so take the opportunity to check food stores, tidy shelves and restock for the new season. An organised pantry will save you money and time at every meal

Love your larder

A larder or pantry – or even a well-stocked and organised cupboard – is your kitchen's fuel store. Ideally, you should be able to rustle up a quick meal from the contents, have piquant ingredients ready to spice up the plainest dish (hello, crispy onions and dried chillies), and be tidy enough to navigate easily.

Traditionally, autumn would have been the time to lay down stocks of food for winter, with pickles and preserves, canned goods and jars of goodies. While that may not be necessary in the age of 24-7 grocery deliveries, there's still value in assessing the food you have in store, clearing out what can't be used (or donating food that you won't eat), and replenishing your supplies.

This seasonal stocktake can help you reduce food waste and shop more efficiently, so you always have the makings of a meal on hand – so go ahead and get organised with our guide!

WALK-IN WONDERS

'Treat a pantry like any other room in your home and consider the end result from an interior design perspective,' says Jaime Frow, founder of Thoughtfully Organised Homes. Jaime suggests choosing a colour palette as you would in any other space in the house, putting up wallpaper, or adding baskets and carefully choosing countertops. 'A functional and beautiful interior can make all the difference to the way you use your larder or pantry, as well as how it makes you feel when you open the doors,' suggests William Durrant, owner of Herringbone kitchens. 'Think shelves, drawers, cold shelves and a stone splashback. Sockets are a must, as both pantries and larders are ideal places to house a toaster or a coffee machine.'

TO DECANT OR NOT?

Whether you have a pull-out larder or a walk-in pantry, organising your storage by decanting foodstuffs into coordinating containers will make your kitchen look more luxurious and create a sense of uniformity and tidiness. But ask yourself whether it's a task you'll be able to stay on top of when life gets busy.

'Decanting into beautiful glass jars always looks picture-perfect on social media but isn't always as neat in reality. It's an extra task after grocery shopping, so won't suit everyone's natural tendencies,' says professional organiser Katherine Blackler, founder of SortMySpace. 'Grains and pastas don't always come in matching volume sizes so you will still need to have an overflow area for the opened packets. And you should decide whether you always empty a jar fully before topping up to ensure you don't leave very old produce at the bottom of the jar.'

STORAGE HACKS FOR PANTRIES

UNDERSHELF BASKET A nifty use of space that's ideal for grab-and-go snacks or folded linens. Try Under-shelf storage basket, Dunelm

STACKABLE CANISTERS Pack up your shelves with square containers that will stack without wobbling. Try The Home Edit & iDesign pantry canister, John Lewis & Partners

TURNTABLE STORAGE Spin the tray to quickly reach sauces and seasoning. Try the Wooden rotating cupboard organiser, A Place for Everything

STEPPED SHELF ORGANISERS Tiered storage means you can easily see any jars and cans at the back of the cupboard. Try Extendable bamboo shelf organiser, Lakeland

SIX-STEP INVENTORY & RESTOCK

1. Empty out all food, check expiry dates and discard or donate anything you can't use or don't enjoy eating.
2. Clean all the shelves and containers, updating your storage options if necessary.
3. Sort supplies into categories, such as pasta, rice and pulses, baking ingredients, cans and jars, spices, and breakfast cereals.
4. Decide which foods you will decant into containers – clear boxes can be stacked inside cupboards; glass jars look good on open shelves; baskets are handy for snack bars.
5. Restock your larder, keeping categories of food in the same place, such as breakfast items or baking ingredients. Put the items you use most front and centre, and consider grouping items into baskets that can be lifted out and put straight onto the table – for example, sauces and condiments.
6. If your larder or pantry is also used to store small appliances, keep heavier items on lower shelves where they will be more accessible. Keep lighter and less-used items, such as tablecloths, on higher shelves. Add a stool for easy access.

Fireside suppers

We're looking forward to colder nights and coming home to crowd-pleasing one-pots

Fireside suppers

LAMB WITH PEPPERS, DATES AND CHICKPEAS

SERVES 6
Use best end of neck chops for a super-tender result with heaps of flavour that also comes in at a great price.

YOU WILL NEED
- 1kg (2¼lb) lamb neck chops
- 3tbsp olive oil ● 1 large onion, finely chopped ● 2 red peppers, sliced
- 4 garlic cloves, crushed ● 1tsp ground coriander ● 1tsp ground cumin
- 1tsp cinnamon ● ½tsp ground ginger ● 400g (14oz) tin chopped tomatoes ● 500ml (1 pint) beef stock
- 2tbsp tomato puree ● 75g (2½oz) pitted dates, roughly chopped
- 2 x 400g (14oz) tins chickpeas, drained and rinsed ● 2tbsp chopped fresh parsley

TO SERVE
- Crusty bread

1. Heat the oven to 160°C/325°F/Gas Mark 3. Season the chops with salt and pepper. Heat half the oil in a large flameproof casserole over a high heat, and fry the lamb in batches for 5 mins until browned. Remove from the pan and set aside. Reduce the heat to low.
2. Add the remaining oil and gently fry the onion, peppers and garlic for 10 mins until soft. Stir in the spices, then fry for a further 1 min. Add the tomatoes, stock, tomato puree, dates and chickpeas, and return the lamb to the pan.
3. Bring to the boil, cover the pan and bake for 2-2½ hrs or until the lamb is tender and falling from the bone. Scatter over the parsley and serve with crusty bread.

Winter Home 33

PORK CHOPS WITH TOMATO & FENNEL SAUCE

SERVES 4

Pork shoulder chops work well here, as they are better suited to a slow cook than loin chops.

YOU WILL NEED

- 4 pork shoulder chops ● 4tbsp extra virgin olive oil ● 1 small onion, chopped ● 1 small head fennel, trimmed and chopped ● 2 garlic cloves, crushed ● 1kg (2¼lb) ripe vine tomatoes, chopped, or 2 x 400g (14oz) tins chopped tomatoes ● 1tsp grated lemon zest ● 1tsp caster sugar ● 2 sprigs fresh sage, bruised ● 2 bay leaves, bruised ● 150g (5¼oz) orzo pasta ● 1tbsp basil leaves

TO SERVE

- Freshly grated Parmesan

1. Heat the oven to 180°C/350°F/Gas Mark 4. Season the chops with salt and pepper. Heat half the oil in a flameproof casserole and brown the chops on both sides for 3-4 mins. Remove the browned pork chops and set aside.
2. Add the remaining oil to the pan and gently fry the onion, fennel and garlic for 10 mins until really soft but not browned. Add the tomatoes, lemon zest, caster sugar, sage and bay leaves, then arrange the chops on top, pressing down into the sauce.
3. Bring the sauce to a simmer, cover the pan and bake for 1 hr. Remove from the oven and carefully stir in the orzo, making sure it's all covered with a little liquid. Cover and bake for a further 10 mins until the orzo is tender. Scatter over the basil leaves and serve with grated Parmesan.

SWEET POTATO, PEPPER AND LENTIL CHILLI

SERVES 4-6

Adding puy lentils instead of mince makes this dish both hearty and healthy.

YOU WILL NEED

- 4tbsp olive oil ● 1 large onion, finely chopped ● 2 garlic cloves, finely chopped ● 2 carrots, finely chopped ● 350g (12¼oz) sweet potatoes, peeled and diced ● 1 red pepper, diced ● 2tsp smoked paprika ● 1tsp ground coriander ● 1tsp chilli powder ● ½tsp ground cumin ● ½tsp ground cinnamon ● 400g (14oz) tin chopped tomatoes ● 500ml (1 pint) vegetable stock ● 2tbsp tomato puree ● 125g (4½oz) puy lentils, washed and dried ● 2 x 400g (14oz) tins kidney beans, drained and rinsed ● 2tbsp chopped fresh coriander

TO SERVE

- Greek yogurt ● Coriander leaves
- Tortilla chips

1. Heat the oil in a large saucepan and gently fry the onion, garlic and a little salt and pepper for 10 mins until soft. Add the carrots, sweet potatoes, red pepper and spices, then fry for a further 5 mins.
2. Add the tomatoes, stock, tomato puree, lentils and kidney beans, and bring to the boil. Lower the heat, cover and simmer gently for 35 mins.
3. Stir in the coriander. Serve with yogurt, tortilla chips and extra coriander.

STICKY CARAMEL CHICKEN

SERVES 4

This is inspired by the addictive flavours of Vietnamese food, where hot/sweet and salty combine perfectly. Serve with rice for a filling supper.

YOU WILL NEED
- 2tbsp vegetable oil ● 8 free-range skin-on chicken thighs ● 4 garlic cloves, finely chopped ● 2tsp freshly grated root ginger ● 1 small onion, finely chopped ● ¼tsp ground black pepper ● 80g (2¾oz) soft brown sugar ● 250ml (8½fl oz) chicken stock ● 4tbsp fish sauce ● 2tbsp light soy sauce

TO SERVE
- Jasmine rice ● Grated carrot
- Coriander leaves ● Sliced red chilli
- Crispy fried shallots ● Lime wedges

1. Heat the oil in a deep, non-stick pan (one with a lid), and brown the chicken pieces over a high heat for approximately 5-6 mins on both sides. Remove from the pan with a slotted spoon, and set aside.
2. Lower the heat and gently fry the garlic, ginger, onion and black pepper for 5 mins until soft. Add the sugar, then stir for 1-2 mins until dissolved. Stir in the stock, fish sauce and soy sauce; bring to a simmer.
3. Return the chicken to the pan, skin side down, cover the pan and cook gently over a low heat for 25 mins. Remove the lid, increase the heat to high and boil the sauce for 10 mins until the chicken is dark brown and the sauce is sticky.
4. Serve the chicken with rice, carrot, chilli, coriander, shallots and lime.

SMOKED FISH AND PRAWN PIE

SERVES 6

This easy fish pie is topped with sliced potatoes rather than the more usual mash, and is lovely and crisp.

YOU WILL NEED
- 75g (2½oz) butter ● 2 leeks, sliced
- 3 sticks celery, sliced ● 40g (1½oz) plain flour ● 50ml (1¾fl oz) milk
- 150ml (5fl oz) soured cream
- 75g (2½oz) mature cheese, grated
- 500g (1lb) smoked haddock fillet, skinned ● 250g (8¾oz) large cooked peeled prawns ● 150g (5¼oz) frozen peas, thawed ● 2tbsp chopped fresh chives ● 750g (1½lb) potatoes, such as King Edwards or Desiree, finely sliced

1. Heat the oven to 200°C/400°F/Gas Mark 6. Melt 50 g (1¾oz) of the butter in a flameproof casserole and fry the leeks and celery for 10 mins until soft but not browned.
2. Stir in the flour and cook for 1 min. Gradually add the milk and soured cream, stirring constantly, until smooth. Bring to the boil, still stirring, and simmer gently for 2 mins until thickened. Remove from the heat, then stir in the cheese. Season to taste.
3. Cut the smoked haddock into bite-size pieces and the prawns in half, if large. Stir the seafood, peas and chives into the leek sauce.
4. Melt the remaining butter and season with a little pepper. Arrange the potato slices over the pie filling, overlapping them. Brush with the melted butter and bake for 40-45 mins until the potatoes are golden and the filling bubbling. Cover with foil if it starts to become too brown. Serve with a green salad.

Nostalgic chocolate puds

Go retro with our old-school favourites

SELF-SAUCING CHOCOLATE PUDDING

SERVES 6

As it bakes, the wet mixture transforms to a gorgeous saucy sponge.

YOU WILL NEED
- 100g (3½oz) butter, softened
- 150g (5¼oz) golden caster sugar
- 3 medium free-range eggs, beaten
- 1tsp vanilla extract
- 125ml (4¼fl oz) whole milk
- 125g (4½oz) self-raising flour
- 30g (1oz) cocoa powder
- 70g (2½oz) dark chocolate, chopped

FOR THE SAUCE
- 100g (3½oz) golden caster sugar
- 25g (¾oz) cocoa powder, sifted

FOR THE PINK CUSTARD
- 35g (1¼oz) sachet strawberry blancmange
- 3tbsp caster sugar
- 500ml (1 pint) whole milk

1. Heat oven to 190°C/375°F/Gas Mark 5. In a large bowl, beat the butter and sugar until light and fluffy. Gradually add the eggs, beating well between each addition. Add the vanilla, then half the milk, flour and cocoa. Stir to combine, then add the remaining milk, flour and cocoa, and the chopped chocolate. Add a pinch of salt, stir then pour the batter into a large ovenproof baking dish and smooth the surface.
2. For the sauce, mix the sugar and cocoa with 300ml (10fl oz) boiling water until smooth, then pour over the batter, being careful not to make any holes in the batter. Bake for 35 mins until a crust forms on the top and there is a slight wobble.
3. For the custard, put the blancmange, sugar and a splash of milk in a pan and briefly whisk until smooth. Gradually pour in the remaining milk while whisking. Cook over a medium heat, stirring for 5 mins or until thickened; transfer to a jug. Serve with plenty of custard.

CHERRY ARCTIC ROLL

SERVES 15

Our boozy berry twist is great for entertaining this winter.

YOU WILL NEED
- 22x34cm (8¾x13½") Swiss roll tin, lined with cling film, overhanging the sides

FOR THE ICE CREAM
- 1 medium free-range egg, separated
- 75g (2¾oz) caster sugar
- 200ml (6¾fl oz) double cream
- 370g (13oz) jar black cherries in kirsch, drained, liquid reserved
- 30g (1oz) dark chocolate, finely chopped

FOR THE CHOCOLATE SPONGE
- 3 medium free-range eggs
- 75g (2¾oz) caster sugar
- 60g (2oz) plain flour
- 20g (¾oz) cocoa powder
- ¼tsp baking powder

1. Start the ice cream 1 day ahead. Using an electric mixer, whisk the egg white with 15g (½oz) sugar to soft peaks. In a separate bowl, whisk the yolk and remaining 60g (2oz) sugar until thick and pale. Add the cream, beating to soft peaks; fold in the egg white.
2. Spoon the ice cream into the middle of the Swiss roll tin (lengthways), in a log shape; freeze for 2 hrs to firm up.
3. Put the cherries and 2tbsp liquid in a food processor; whizz until smooth. Swirl the chocolate and 100g (3½oz) of the cherry mix through the ice cream to create a ripple. Freeze for a further 2 hrs. Chill remaining cherry mixture and reserved liquid.
4. Using the cling film, mould the ice cream into a neat log the length of the tin, twisting the ends; freeze overnight.
5. The next day, heat the oven to 200°C/400°F/Gas Mark 6. Line the tin with baking paper.
6. For the sponge, whisk eggs and sugar until thickened. Fold in flour, cocoa, baking powder. Pour into the tin; bake for 8 mins.
7. Flip the sponge on to a wire rack to cool. Peel away the paper, then brush one side with 4tbsp of reserved cherry liquid.
8. Transfer to baking paper, soaked side down. Spread with the remaining cherry mixture. Unwrap the ice cream, put in centre of the sponge; roll up then freeze, seam side down, until ready to serve.

Winter Home 39

CHOCOLATE RICE PUDDING WITH PEAR COMPOTE

SERVES 4-6

All the comfort of an old-fashioned rice pudding with a rich, indulgent and hearty twist.

YOU WILL NEED
- 50g (1¾oz) unsalted butter • 50g (1¾oz) dark brown soft sugar • ¼tsp ground cinnamon • 200g (7oz) pudding rice • 410g (14½oz) tin evaporated milk • 300ml (10fl oz) whole milk • 100g (3½oz) 70% dark chocolate, chopped • 100g (3½oz) crème fraîche

FOR THE PEARS
- Juice 1 orange, plus 2 strips pared rind, finely sliced • 25g (¾oz) caster sugar • 1tsp vanilla bean paste • 2-3 pears, peeled, each cut into 6 wedges

1. Put the butter and dark brown soft sugar in a medium pan over a high heat. Bring to a fierce bubble and stir in a pinch of salt, the cinnamon and rice. Turn the heat to low, add the evaporated milk, whole milk and 150ml (5fl oz) water, then simmer for 45 mins, stirring regularly. If it starts to catch, add a splash of water or milk.
2. Remove from heat, add 75g (2¾oz) chocolate, stir until combined and leave to stand for 5 mins. Scatter the remaining chocolate over the top, stir briefly and leave for 1 min to allow puddles of chocolate to form.
3. Meanwhile, mix the orange juice with enough water to make up 150ml (5fl oz) and set aside. Put the sugar in a medium pan over a high heat and caramelise without stirring. As soon as the sugar is liquid and amber coloured, pour in the orange juice mixture, orange rind and vanilla. Bring to a simmer, add the pears; cover and simmer over a low-to-medium heat for 10 mins.
4. Using a slotted spoon, remove the pears and set aside. Simmer the syrup, uncovered, for 5-10 mins until reduced by half. Take off the heat and add the pears.
5. Serve the rice pudding with the pears in their syrup, plus strands of orange rind and crème fraîche.

POSITIVE OUTCOME

Decluttering is not just about what you decide to let go, but also what you keep – and can therefore celebrate and enjoy

How to get rid of emotional clutter

Winter is a great time to do a clear out, but are you finding it hard to let go? Our experts advise…

Some belongings come with deep emotional ties to a person or time in your past (or both). You want to stay connected to them, but they might be swamping your space or stopping you from embracing the now and finding happiness in the present.

There are myriad ways to streamline and tidy your home, but we asked three professional organisers with expertise and experience in the psychological aspects of decluttering for their advice on how to get rid of emotional clutter.

Cher Casey of The Mindful Organiser reveals, 'The most common categories of "emotional" clutter that I see are kids' artwork, clothes and toys, items passed down by deceased family members, things from a person's childhood or a meaningful occasion or life stage (wedding, uni or pre-divorce), and jewellery. Books can be an underdog category, but are highly sentimental for many of my clients.'

Tanya Sanyal at Organised Joy adds, 'It might be about emotions attached to certain items, or about shopping behaviours or habits that have led to the clutter. For example, overbuying groceries and stocking up on bulk deals may be linked to a feeling of scarcity growing up or an excessive fear of crises. Without unpicking the possible emotional causes of clutter, it's hard to deal with the physical issue.'

Before you start decluttering, Cher warns that this process must be undertaken carefully. 'Highly emotional and sentimental items should be considered in the latter stages of a decluttering journey,' she says. 'Decluttering is like a muscle – the more you do it, the easier it becomes to make conscious decisions about keeping or releasing something. I usually begin with functional, non-sentimental things, such as utensils, groceries, medicine and household cleaners, to help clients feel comfortable making confident decisions. We can then move to other items, such as clothes and linens, before working our way up to sentimental possessions.

'I also remind clients that decluttering is equally about what you keep and celebrate, not just what you release,' Cher continues. 'I empower them to curate their space by selecting and showcasing items with happy memories of people they love, and letting go of painful or sad memories.'

Here, we explore the ways in which you can tackle this type of clutter at home, freeing yourself from any emotional ties, while simultaneously clearing your surroundings.

TRUST THE PROCESS

After sorting out functional, non-sentimental items, move on to clothes and shoes

1 PASS ON UNWANTED GIFTS

Julze Best, professional organiser at Holistic Home and Wellbeing, advises, 'If a gift you are keeping out of obligation lowers your energy, cherish the sentiment in which it was given and pass it on to someone else to enjoy. Ask yourself how often has anyone ever enquired where a gift they gave you is, or why it's not on display?'

2 PHOTOGRAPH HEIRLOOMS THAT AREN'T YOUR STYLE

Julze adds, 'If you don't like a family heirloom that has been given to you, don't feel obliged to keep it just because it belonged to Granny! If you want to remember an item, photograph it, then gift or sell it and treat yourself to something more pleasing that gives you a positive reminder of your relative.'

3 DO A TRIAL DECLUTTER FOR SENTIMENTAL MEMENTOES

Nostalgia can make this a tricky one, especially if you're prone to decision fatigue. Cher says, 'I'd approach this in the same manner as you would the belongings of a deceased person, such as talking about the items with your family and seeing if someone else might appreciate them more. 'For many, a trial declutter can be a very impactful way to emotionally detach from sentimental things,' Cher continues. 'Separate the most cherished items and box up the rest for, say, three or six months. This allows you to experience life without these items in your vicinity. You can revisit them and see if their attachment has changed with time.'

4 ORGANISE AND EDIT PHOTO COLLECTIONS

Cher says that photos, whether printed or digital, can be more straightforward. 'You can reduce a collection of photographs by letting go of blurry, damaged or duplicate images, and categorising them. Or giving some to other family members, putting them into photo albums or digitising them for easier storage.' Another option would be to create a photo gallery wall. 'Once revised and edited, it can be a really nice family activity to look through a collection of photos with loved ones,' Cher says. 'It can give you the chance to relive memories together and to identify unknown people or places.'

5 MIND YOUR LANGUAGE ABOUT A LOST LOVED ONE'S BELONGINGS

'I am very selective in the language I use when decluttering emotional items,' says Cher. 'I never say the words "bin", "throw away" or "get rid". Instead I use gentle phrases, such as "let go", "release", "re-home" and "pass on". No one wants to think they're "getting rid" of their mum's china set, even if they don't like it and have no use for it. People are often able to let go of sentimental items if they know the objects are going to be used and loved by others.'

6 TALK YOUR WAY THROUGH DIFFICULT DECLUTTER DECISIONS

Cher continues, 'When clients have a lot of one particular category – for example, their deceased parent's or partner's clothes – we'll look at items together and talk about their loved one. In doing so, this often allows them to be more selective in what they keep, such as their dad's favourite jacket.' 'When grief is involved, decluttering needs to be done gently and always when the grieving person is ready. It's a terrible feeling to let go when you're deep in grief,' Cher says. 'I invite them to tell me about their loved one. I listen and I hold space for people to cry and laugh, and feel other emotions. This is key to emotionally processing and ultimately releasing sentimental items. Decluttering is where tidying meets therapy.' Tanya adds, 'Getting a really good idea of what outcome they want from the process is crucial before starting to go through items. It can be the guiding North Star that will motivate them.'

7 SEE A COLLECTION IN A NEW LIGHT

Over time, a collection can get out of control and become more of a burden than a pleasure. Tanya says, 'I would ask questions to help clients decide for themselves if their collection is truly bringing them joy, considering an overall vision of their ideal lifestyle.' 'Once we understand the purpose and value of the collection in that context, we would then take all the items and lay them out somewhere new,' she says. 'This is because when we constantly see a collection together, our mind may no longer see it as individual pieces but as a cohesive whole.' 'I would then encourage a client to pick their favourite items in their collection, the pieces that they 100 per cent love,' Tanya says, 'and use that as a benchmark to measure the rest.'

STREAMLINED KITCHEN

Bulk-buying groceries can be linked to a fear of crisis, but this can be worked through

How to get rid of emotional clutter

SHOWCASE MEMORIES

By decluttering objects with unhappy links, you can focus on the items that spark joy

A PLACE FOR EVERYTHING

The more you declutter, the easier it becomes to make decisions about keeping or releasing

Tidy up time

The secret to a beautiful home is plenty of storage to hide away clutter, so find a place for everything with our round-up of the best solutions

FEATURE HOLLY REANEY

Tidy up time

DUAL SEATING

OPPOSITE When space is limited, including fitted furniture, such as a window seat, can prove invaluable. 'Utilising each nook and cranny can free up space you never knew you had,' explains Rachal Hutcheson, national retail manager at Sharps. 'Not only does fitted furniture help you to keep a room tidy, but it often adds value to your home if you decide to move on.'

LARDER LOVE

LEFT Open shelves offer a lighter alternative to fitted cabinetry, but keeping them tidy is vital. 'To avoid an overly cluttered look, display everyday essentials. Regularly used crockery and glassware, and glass jars containing your most-used dry ingredients, will keep the space organised while also making it easier to clean,' says Amy McSorley, product development director at Nkuku. Jars and tableware from Nkuku.

OUTSIDE THE BOX

BELOW LEFT Shoe storage can often pose a problem. While a hallway can house your day-to-day pairs, occasional or seasonal footwear can be more difficult to store. Disguised as a blanket box, this bench from Cotswold Company opens to reveal eight shoe compartments, and is topped with a cushioned seat for added functionality.

STILL STANDING

BELOW The humble bookshelf shouldn't be overlooked when it comes to storage solutions. Create a visually appealing display by combining decorative items with practical elements, such as pretty boxes, vases and books. For added storage potential, opt for a bookshelf with integrated drawers, like this Laura Ashley Balmoral design from Next.

Winter Home 47

BUILDING UP

LEFT Make the most of otherwise dead space by framing a doorway with bookshelves, as seen in this beautiful design by Laura Stephens. Not only does it provide plentiful storage for books but the colourful spines will add a burst of character to this often overlooked spot.

BEHIND CLOSED DOORS

BELOW Nearly every living room features a television, however, they aren't renowned for their beauty, especially when you take into account additional boxes and wiring. Concealing your television in a dresser greatly reduces the visual clutter and provides a more harmonious living space. Featured is the small armoire TV cabinet, from Susie Watson Designs.

ON THE SIDE

BELOW LEFT Combining hidden storage with a decorative platform, sideboards are a valuable addition to any room of the home. When it comes to styling the top, cut the clutter by opting for items of different heights and textures that can be arranged in an artful trio – such as the flowers, lamp and small vase showcased on this Mara sideboard from Barker & Stonehouse.

HIDDEN TREASURES

RIGHT While they may have seen their last holiday, vintage trunks and suitcases still have plenty of life left when it comes to décor. Beautifully constructed and brimming with historic charm, they can be stacked to create an effective visual display. Fill each case with seasonal clothing, spare bedlinen or other occasionally used items for an attractive alternative to storage boxes.

FULLY UTILISED

RIGHT An essential partner to open-plan living, a functional space – whether that is a utility, boot room or a combination of the two – will help to keep the key living areas of your home clutter-free. When designing a utility or boot room, think about the task it needs to perform and do an inventory of what you want to store. Whether opting for built-in cabinetry, such as this from Olive & Barr, or assembling your own, combine shelving, hooks and seating to ensure the utmost flexibility. Baskets are a great complement to cubbyholes, helping you to keep ephemera neatly contained.

OUT OF SIGHT

BELOW Endlessly versatile, tall cupboards can be used for everything from a compact library to a linen cabinet. 'The cupboard's height not only optimises storage, but it also minimises the footprint making it a space-saving solution for any room,' says Paul Staden, founder and designer at Pilgrim House. Try their handmade New-Shaker tall cupboard in Appleterre.

ADD CHARACTER

BELOW RIGHT Combine storage with sustainability by opting for secondhand pieces. From traditional dressers and bureaus to blanket boxes and drawers, Restored by Betel, as its name suggests, breathes new life into old pieces. Under expert guidance, each piece of furniture is transformed by people who are also working to turn their lives around – so your purchase is not only good for the planet but good for the community, too. Old Charm court cupboard.

Warming drinks

Stay toasty this winter with five creative hot drinks that you can make at home

MULLED WINE

On a festive winter's evening there isn't anything much better than a warm, spicy, sweet mug of mulled wine to warm you. In a large saucepan mix a bottle of red wine with the peel of one large orange (avoiding the pith), the juice of the orange, a 6cm (2.5") piece of root ginger peeled and sliced, one cinnamon stick, four cloves and demerara sugar to taste. Cover and heat on a medium heat until the mixture is hot, but not boiling, then leave on a low heat for at least an hour to let the spices infuse. Strain and serve with a splash of brandy if desired.

MULLED CIDER

Keep warm on Bonfire Night with a deliciously toasty mulled cider. Pour a litre of decent traditional cider into a saucepan on a low heat and let it warm through for a minute. Add three cloves, two star anise, ¼ nutmeg grated into the pan, a cinnamon stick, a vanilla pod cut in half lengthways, the juice of one orange and one clementine, as well as one pomegranate into the pot. Turn the heat up and once it is boiling bring the heat back down and leave to simmer for around eight minutes. Add some caster sugar if you like it sweeter then strain to serve.

GINGERBREAD COFFEE

Add a little spice to your next caffeine hit with this festive drink. Make a spice mixture using 175g black treacle, ½ teaspoon of bicarbonate of soda, four tablespoons of dark-brown, soft sugar, one teaspoon of ground ginger, and ¾ of a tablespoon of cinnamon. Mix all of the ingredients together then leave in the fridge for ten minutes. This will be enough spice mix for six drinks. Brew some fresh coffee and mix around 50 millilitres of it with a sixth of the spice mixture in a mug until everything has dissolved. Fill the rest of the mug with coffee, top with single cream to taste and a generous squirt of whipped cream. Finish with a dusting of ground clove.

APPLE AND CINNAMON TODDY

Fight illness with this twist on a classic. Mix one litre of unsweetened apple juice with two tablespoons of clear honey and 25g of raisins in a saucepan, then add a cinnamon stick and six cloves. Leave to settle for around an hour. Peel and core a dessert apple and cut into four rings. Place the saucepan over a low heat, add the apple rings and simmer for 20 minutes. Remove the cinnamon and cloves then stir in two tablespoons of lemon juice. Split between four glass mugs with a ring of apple in each. If you want to give it a bit of a kick you could add a measure of brandy to each glass, too.

PARISIAN HOT CHOCOLATE

Indulge yourself with a rich, intense, grown-up hot chocolate that is best served in an espresso cup. In a saucepan stir ¼ cup of cocoa with two tablespoons of granulated sugar and a generous pinch of salt. Now stir in a litre of whole milk, 280g of quality milk chocolate and 60g of 60% dark (bittersweet) chocolate. Heat over a medium heat until the chocolate melts and the mixture is hot. Whisk until it thickens and forms a decadent mixture. Serve between six small mugs.

Rustic retreat

Create cosy, cabin-inspired spaces, perfect for hibernating in this winter, by decorating with natural materials, earthy tones and organic textures

HUNKER DOWN
At the heart of every cosy cabin is a relaxing living space. Iliv's Chalet collection features textural printed and woven fabrics, from ikat and kilim designs to brushed checks and stripes, perfect for layering for warmth and softness. Available in eight colour stories, including the Rouge colourway pictured, 'combine with metallic accents in light fixtures and cabinet hardware, and finish with accessories such as antler décor and nature-themed artwork,' advises Debbie Leigh, design manager. Sofa in Chalet; curtains and blinds in Courchevel; cushions in various fabrics from the range.

Rustic retreat

MOUNTAIN VIEWS
Wood-clad walls are synonymous with the cabin look but instead embrace a beautiful alpine-themed wallpaper. Inspired by Galtür, a pretty mountain village in Austria's Tyrol region, this design from Mind the Gap would look wonderful as a feature wall. 'The background features a rich amber that brings the warmth and colour of a wooden lodge – pair with deep forest greens and highlights of sky blue for an authentic and inviting feel,' advises Stefan Ormenisan, founder and creative director. Galtür of Tyrol wallpaper in Amber Gold; Winston Tufted sofa in Cambridge Sage leather, both Mind the Gap.

Given today's technology-saturated world, the idea of retreating to a remote cabin to reconnect with nature has never been more appealing. From alpine chalets and mountain lodges to Scandinavian lakeside homes, there is plenty of inspiration when it comes to cosy cabin style.

Conjuring up visions of timber-clad buildings set in sweeping rural vistas, cabins appeal to our sense of wanderlust and adventure. With humble beginnings as rudimentary, functional shelters, they have evolved across the centuries to become permanent residences and boutique stays. 'When the pandemic stopped a lot of overseas travel, a variety of unique rural retreats popped up for those looking for an alternative to holidays abroad. The idea of switching off our phones and living off-grid in a rustic cabin or lodge sounded heavenly – surrounded by beautifully crafted objects and forests to go on long ambles,' explains Jessica Hanley, founder of Piglet in Bed. 'Fast forward to today, and the romance of this way of living is manifesting itself as a contemporary lifestyle trend that people are bringing into their own homes,' she adds.

Inside, cabins have warmth and rustic charm at their core. They offer an inviting escape to the dramatic landscapes that surround them, while also reflecting the beautiful tones and textures of nature. Timber-clad walls, crackling fires, warm, earthy colours, distressed surfaces and a plethora of cosy textures are signature features of the look, but perhaps most notable is the use of natural materials. 'To achieve the "cabincore" aesthetic, embrace materials that evoke the textures found in the wilderness. Incorporate stone, reclaimed wood, linen and wool to add depth and rustic appeal,' explains Jessica Hanley.

However, you don't need to have an authentic timber cabin to create a captivating hygge ambience. 'Cladding an urban interior in wood might be a step too far,' suggests Stefan Ormenisan, founder and creative director of Mind the Gap. Instead 'rich wool textiles such as bouclé cushions and plaid throws layered together on wooden or leather furniture alongside an atmospheric wallpaper will add to the laid-back feeling of a cabin interior.'

When designing a cabin-style space you can't underestimate the role of cosy fabrics and this season there are plenty of collections that tap into the tactile trend. Mixing different prints and patterns is a brilliant way to create a homely look, but for ultimate cosiness, it is all about textures – think woollens and chunky weaves teamed with slubby linen, bouclé and sheepskin. 'Expect to see plenty of loopy textures and touchy-feely fabrics coming through,' says Nicky Line, chief product officer at Loaf. 'Our new Shearer sheepskin range of soft furnishings hits the sweet spot of comfort.'

Colour palette-wise, look to nature for inspiration; earthy schemes of browns and warm neutrals are a go-to, but blues and greens can beautifully complement the honeyed hues of wood and stone. 'Stick to warm and rich tones like chestnut browns, fern greens, and more neutral oatmeals,' says Jessica Hanley. 'These colours create a soothing atmosphere reminiscent of the outdoors. Deep berries and cranberry reds pair particularly well with more earthy tones.'

SNUGGLE UP
After returning from a long winter walk, there is nothing like curling up in a comfortable armchair by the fire with a hot drink. This Smooch love seat sofa bed from Loaf oozes comfort with its loose feather-back cushions and sumptuous curves. Pictured in the rich Quince Jam Clever Vintage linen, it would make a warming centrepiece for a living room and shines here set against rustic panelling in dusky blueish-grey. Style it with Easy Squish cushions in complementary berry tones. 'Colours like reds and damsons can be both playful and sophisticated and are easy to layer onto neutrals,' says Nicky Line.

WONDER WALLS
Small rooms can be tricky to decorate, but are also a great place to introduce pattern. Ornate wallpaper will not only add softness and elegance to small bathrooms, but it can also distract from their compact size. With its stylised floral design, this Arts and Crafts Trent wallpaper in River Wandle from Morris & Co pairs perfectly with cabin-style wooden flooring and linen basin curtain. 'For the Emery Walker's House wallpapers, we focused on emulating the rich, warming colourways found in the originals, and I think that works so well in smaller, cabin spaces,' says Morris & Co's lead designer Jessica Clayworth.

LAYERED LIVING
The ultimate winter sanctuary calls for plenty of cosy bedding to hibernate under on chilly nights. 'When it comes to pattern, integrate heritage checks, which we often associate with cabins, into your décor through bedding, cushions and upholstery,' advises Jessica Hanley, founder of Piglet in Bed. 'Checks and gingham will add a cosy, nostalgic touch to your space. With bedding, it's all about layers – brushed cotton or linen sheets, merino wool duvets, and chunky knit blankets.' Olive brushed cotton bedding bundle; Burnt Orange Check cabin wool blanket; Berry Gingham linen quilt, all Piglet in Bed.

BALANCING ACT
Colour drenching a kitchen in a dark hue is a daring move, but it can feel wonderfully cocooning and cosy, especially in smaller kitchens. Introduce warm, natural materials and metallic finishes to keep it inviting. In this kitchen by Devol, the deep Pantry Blue walls and cabinets are paired with a mix of staved iroko and copper worktops, copper wall lights and splashback. 'Wood is beautifully tactile and naturally warmer to the touch than stone, so it offers a more relaxed look on worktops, ideal for kitchens that blend into living areas,' says Helen Parker, creative director.

FOLKSY FABRICS

LEFT Bringing together textile traditions from across the globe, from Indian ikats to the suzanis of Uzbekistan, Lewis & Wood's Travel Trunk fabrics are perfect for adding a bohemian, homely touch to rustic spaces. Comprising mostly linens, the fabric designs have a beautiful varied texture, which complements the patina of natural stone and timber, and they are available in an array of warm earthy colours, including Ginger, Henna, Raffia, Cocoa and Walnut. Fabrics on cushions from left: Minna Maze linen in Ginger; Totem linen blend in Russet; Womad LG 100 linen in Henna; Kanthakat cotton in Dark Ginger; seat cushion in Jakarta linen in Ebony, all from Lewis & Wood.

GATHER AROUND

BOTTOM LEFT Bench seating is becoming increasingly popular in kitchen-dining areas as it creates a relaxed feel for social gatherings. Perfect for a compact cosy cabin space, this built-in seating-cum-storage unit in Smoked Oak timber from Husk creates a cocooning feel when combined with the Smoked Oak Groove wall panelling. 'Husk customises standard Ikea Bestå units to create built-in seating that can be plain wood or upholstered. This clever hack makes it affordable and practical as the design includes deep drawers, perfect for hiding away clutter,' says Dave Young, founder of Husk kitchens. Complete the rustic cabin look with antique stick-back Windsor dining chairs, jute rugs and a muted linen tablecloth and cushions.

HOME AND DRY

RIGHT If space allows, having a separate boot room is a sought-after feature of any rural home. Floor-to-ceiling cabinetry, wall shelving and wall-mounted hooks will offer ample storage while saving valuable floor space, and a cushioned bench is always handy for kicking off muddy boots. Wood panelling and woven storage baskets will enhance the cabin aesthetic, while reclaimed terracotta or quarry floor tiles are hardwearing but will also bring warmth and texture. The Hambledon umbrella stand and small welly stand, and Brading rectangular basket in small and large, are all available from Garden Trading.

Rustic retreat

Fill your home with books

Literature lover? A home library or reading nook could be the escape from everyday life that you've been waiting for…

Despite our constantly 'switched-on' digital lives, it appears we're still very much in love with old-fashioned, physical books. And it's not just the joy of finding somewhere quiet to read them that we love – we're talking surrounding ourselves with books to create libraries in our homes.

And there's hard evidence singing the praises of home libraries. Children who come from homes with books do better in school, and in general life, than those without. A recent survey of 160,000 adults in 31 countries concluded that teens growing up in a home with a sizeable home library (at least 80 books) has a large effect on literacy in later life. The paper, titled *Scholarly Culture: How Books in Adolescence Enhance Adult Literacy, Numeracy and Technology Skills in 31 Societies*, discovered that teenagers with only lower levels of secondary education, but who grew up surrounded by books, 'became as literate, numerate and technologically apt in adulthood as university graduates who grew up with only a few books.'

Housing 80+ books, though, could be a bit of a spatial challenge. Sales of bookshelves were reportedly up 10 per cent in 2018, but what if you want to do something more creative with your collection, like the understair libraries you keep pinning on Pinterest? Adding a home library or reading nook could be the answer, as interior designer and project manager Anna Auzins (annaauzins.co.uk) points out. 'I think the need for the tangible has increased. We're realising that we could end up living in sterile boxes if we aren't careful. Books make a room feel very homely; they ground it and make it feel like someone actually lives there.

'Some people are fortunate enough to have a whole room for books, which is glorious, but these often form part of complete house renovation projects. One project I worked on involved building in the shelving and adding cornicing, so the bookcases look part of the walls. On another project, the couple had 12,000 books to house! But I've also worked on projects where the library just forms a corner of a room. In one 1930s house, the kitchen had been extended at the back to form a big kitchen-dining-family room, which left the former dining part of the room redundant. By putting in shelving, it became a space in its own right.'

Window seats, snugs and TV-free living spaces are all options you can consider when looking to create quiet zones, especially if you're planning a big reconfiguration of the interior of your home.

'The projects we work on can vary from a multifunctional space with storage, like an integrated desk with a bookcase, to a grand library with floor-to-ceiling shelving, which may require its own access ladder,' says Cari Bateman, senior designer at Neville Johnson (nevillejohnson.co.uk). 'Many of our clients who embrace the digital age still have a passion for books.'

'Books are decoration in their own right, adding colour and texture to a room,' Anna says. 'When you introduce shelving for books, it means you aren't just looking at a blank wall – you're looking at life. A library creates warmth; a place to de-stress and detox and allow our minds to think in a different way.'

Content creator and book-lover Bronte Huskinson (@bookishbronte) agrees. 'In my house, books are everywhere,' she says. 'I love the idea of making a little reading den with plenty of fairy lights, blankets – and unlimited cups of tea, of course!'

So how do you go about creating your dream home library? Anna, who confesses to 'squeezing bookshelves into tiny areas' wherever she's lived, believes you can put a 'library' anywhere. 'All you need are some shelves, a comfortable, decent chair and lighting, which means at least one power point,' she explains. 'You could be fancy and use lighting to highlight the shelves and the books, which looks great.' What's key though, is that the shelves have to be able to take the weight of the books that are going on them. 'Any good joiner should be able to advise,' she adds. 'I once fitted 3.5m-long floating shelves, but in order to make sure they were up to the job, we built in discreet "bookends" mid-shelf to help take the weight.' When shopping for a bookcase, Anna recommends one with height-adjustable shelves to avoid having that one book that just won't fit.

'I love using wood veneer,' she continues, 'but painted MDF is much more cost-effective. I usually make shelves 30cm deep, but you can choose 20cm-deep ones for paperbacks.' Anna also encourages her clients to be brave with colour in their home libraries. 'It will make you stop and pause,' she explains. 'Try painting the back of the shelves a bold colour, so you see a hint of it through the books.'

'Think about using empty, unused wall space in your home for shelving,' says Cari, 'like the space under your stairs. Fitted furniture allows you to create personalised storage that works for you, creating a sophisticated and clutter-free environment in the process. By incorporating bookcases in areas around a door frame or in an awkward alcove, you don't only make use of wasted space, but the feature can become an attractive and integral focal point to the room.'

'The home libraries I find most interesting are the ones you find in unusual places, like books going up the stairs, surrounding the bed or around the TV,' adds Bronte. 'And I just love it when people fill whole walls with books. I have a bookshelf in my living room, but my collection has long since outgrown that. Many of my books are piled up in corners of rooms because of the lack of space for another bookshelf. The piles have almost become features in their own right!' she laughs. 'There are always books wherever you look.'

'Home libraries can be about more than just books,' says Anna. 'Try interspersing books with photos, or favourite toys the kids have outgrown. Or display something collected on holiday – it adds to the life of it all.'

Book keep

Sew these quick-stitch bookmarks so you won't lose your place

YOU WILL NEED
- 3 patterned cotton fat quarters
- Thin fusible interfacing
- Matching thread
- Ruler, cutting mat and rotary cutter

1 From each patterned fabric and the interfacing, measure and cut a 10cm (4") square.
2 Fuse the interfacing to the wrong side of one of the fabric squares. Take another of the fabric squares and fold it in half along the diagonal, with wrong sides together, to form a triangle.
3 Stack the interfaced square with right sides up, top with the triangle piece, followed by the final fabric square, with right sides down.
4 Pin and sew the layers together around the edge with a 5mm (¼") seam allowance. Leave a 5cm (2") gap along one side for turning through.
5 Trim the corners and turn right sides out. Fold the gap edges under by 5mm (¼") and press. Topstitch all the way around to finish.

Recharging at home

Enthusiasm for having your own at-home retreat is on the rise, from art studios to reading nooks, garden cabins to spa bathrooms. But why do we need that emotional room to escape to, asks Jennifer Morgan?

Recharging at home

Our homes are our sanctuaries, but ever feel like you need more? A space you can escape to within the confines of its boundaries, where you can recharge and reset? Well, it seems you're not alone.

It's a growing trend, which the team at Pinterest identified back in 2022 as one to watch. 'We predicted that people would plan their own great escapes at home, with searches for "crystal rooms", "home massage rooms" and "tiny library rooms" all seeing large increases,' says Matt Siberry, head of home at Pinterest UK. 'We've all been through a lot over the past few years, with mental wellness top of the agenda, and many of us are spending more time in our homes now. I think it's even more important that people can create a haven at home. Whether that's a room dedicated to a favourite hobby or a cosy corner, the main thing is that it provides an emotional release.'

Catherine Hallissey, a chartered psychologist (catherinehallissey.com), agrees: 'We are taking in more information than ever, so it's essential that we have a space to down tools and rest our bodies and minds. Spending time in your personal retreat should feel like an oasis in your busy life, a place to rest your body and mind and soothe your soul.'

'I have a busy life running my own business,' says Lisa Ingram of LittleLeaf Organic (littleleaforganic.com), who sell cotton bedlinen, pyjamas, babywear and homeware. 'Plus I have a family of four, almost grown-up, kids. So those few hours when I can escape from the hectic busyness of everyday life and retreat to my pottery studio are very precious to me.' Lisa, who's been a part-time potter for 30 years, says that in her studio, she's on her own, 'which is such a rarity'. Her studio is a part of the garage. 'It's even got a woodburning stove,' she says. 'The concentration involved in making pottery (or any sort of craft) means that your mind can't get distracted by problems or issues and you become fully focused on what you're doing.'

Fellow artist Helen Stone (helenstoneart.com) agrees: 'My mindset changes the minute I step into my studio at home. Most of the time I'm juggling and trying to fit things in here, there, and everywhere, but there's a singular focus when I'm making art – when it's just me, my ideas, and a sense of creative purpose.' Helen admits that it took a while for her to realise that she needed a place to escape to for her art. 'It makes such a difference. My easel is ready whenever I am, and I swear time runs differently in the studio – it goes so fast.'

While Helen's happy-at-home space is creative, others are much more chilled. 'Everyone's escape space will vary,' explains Catherine Hallissey, 'but there are a few key factors that are common to all. The key thing to focus on is how you feel in the space – it's not just a case of somewhere looking good, it needs to feel good too. I'd suggest taking a sensory approach to creating your own happy space. When you look around your space, do you feel relaxed? Does it feel cosy? Are the scents relaxing or uplifting? Are the sounds soothing? Can you maximise natural light?' Catherine also says to clear away as much clutter as possible, creating a space where you can unwind.

'During lockdown, many people realised that open-plan spaces were not ideal when a room must serve multiple functions,' she explains. 'Instead, it feels much cosier to create little nooks designated to different activities. Reading nooks are especially popular, such as a cosy chair in front of a window where you can feel the warmth of the winter sun.'

At-home retreats also mean that you don't need to pack up and go anywhere when you need

respite. Sara Bird, stylist and author of *Retreats for the Soul* (Ryland Peters & Small), says such a retreat offers 'instant value, a place that's good to go and can be used without too much fuss.' In her book, she visits hideaways and havens at the bottom of gardens, on the water and in the wild. Sara says: 'Retreats are a place to have quality "me-time", whether this is via a hobby or something more of a mindful experience – a sheltered spot to view nature, somewhere restful to close one's eyes, or even some place to shift and shuffle interior décor or possessions. It's a setting to do something which isn't a chore.'

Brand and art photographer Carla Watkins (carlawatkins.com) has been creating her own retreat at home, turning her spare room into a 'library/campervan/narrowboat hybrid', as she describes it. 'I had plans to buy my own campervan, but after buying my first home, funds were tight, so I decided to create my own mini-holiday destination at home instead,' she says. The room has lots of bookshelves for Carla's many books (she's an ex-librarian), as well as a sofa bed where she sleeps while on her mini breaks. She also lives fairly near the sea, so she heads to the beach for the day as part of her 'getaway'.

'We can use a retreat to close the door on one experience and open another to something new,' agrees Sara Bird, 'giving us the chance to reset. A retreat can introduce fresh insights, allow solace in a secure place, encourage us to explore or be at ease with contented characteristics.' Sara believes that our retreats often have 'touchpoints', things which are meaningful or personally valuable. 'In physical terms, it could be a favourite heirloom chair, a fabric remnant from the past, or personal pieces which rekindle childhood memories. The senses have a cherished presence too – a scented candle can instantly bring back early recollections, while a sound can connect you to a time and place.'

Over at Pinterest, Matt Siberry has noticed a surge in search for "home spa bathrooms" and "shower room aesthetic ideas" as people look for ways to create that calming sanctuary at home. 'Spa-like bathroom routines and calming showers let you switch off from the world, connect with your thoughts and truly enjoy some much needed me time,' he says. 'Everyone needs a break sometimes, and an emotional escape room is a space where you can truly relax and connect with your own feelings. It's an at-home retreat to decompress and recharge.'

'My studio really is my happy place, a sanctuary which genuinely helps me de-stress and lifts my mood,' explains Lisa Ingram. 'I find myself smiling as soon as I start to climb the stairs to it – which I've painted in bright rainbow colours!'

'Most of the time I'm juggling to fit things in, but when I'm making art in my studio, it's just me, my ideas, and a sense of creative purpose'

Haddon **cabinets** in Mallard Green, Kitchen Makers

Cosy corner

These simple design steps are all you need to ensure your reading nook (or box-set bolthole) is the serene spot you're after

Cosy corner

HEAVY CURTAINS

ABOVE LEFT Swap out your voiles or lightweight curtains for a thick, heavy pair to dress your windows for winter. Not only will they help insulate the room and keep cold draughts out, they'll also help with soundproofing, so lashing rain or howling wind shouldn't disturb you while you're curled up.
Curtains2go or Dunelm for lots of budget-friendly thermal-lined options

LAYERED RUGS

ABOVE RIGHT A thick wool rug underfoot will keep toes toasty and help with any chills coming up through floorboards. For an extra level of comfort, layer a smaller rug of a different texture, such as a sheepskin, on top. The rugs on top can be small, so they're easier to swap out come summer.
Try Weaver Green for sustainable rugs made using plastic bottles

PANELLING

RIGHT Wood panelling is a great way to add texture to your space and give the room a bit more depth. Wide, rustic panels can be attached directly to your wall and can be painted or left bare, with just a coat of matt varnish for protection.
Visit WallpaperDirect to cheat the look of wood panelling

Winter Home

SOFT CANDLELIGHT

ABOVE LEFT The glow from flickering candles is a must-have when creating a nook for snuggling up in. Tealights in votives or pillar candles in glass lanterns will create a calm atmosphere. If you've young children, battery options or fairy lights offer a safer option.
Try Nkuku for stunning glass lanterns

COMFY CUSHIONS

ABOVE RIGHT When it comes to cushions, more is definitely more! Mix up your sizes, shapes and textures, from oversized velvets to linen-covered bolsters and faux fur or mohair miniatures. Plus a couple of blankets and throws on hand are perfect for chillier evenings.
Check out Bronte By Moon for gorgeous mohair and more

MOOD LIGHTING

LEFT For reading or crafting you might need a little more illumination. Floor-standing reading lamps, low-hung pendants or dimmable side lights are all good options, but make sure you choose warm-white bulb, so your space still feels cosy and intimate.
Pooky has some amazing base and shade options, plus rechargeable portable lamps

All ablaze

Create a natural alternative to shop-bought firelighters and fill your home with beautiful seasonal scents

YOU WILL NEED
- Soy wax pellets
- Cupcake baking tray
- Cupcake cases
- Dried flowers
- Dried herbs
- Cinnamon sticks
- Dried orange slices
- Soy wicks

Winter is the season of the fireplace – its heat and gently flickering flames are key to creating a cosy atmosphere. Whether you have an open fire or a modern log burner, these firelighters will fill your living room with sweet fragrance.

1 Preheat the oven to 170°C/325°F/Gas Mark 3 and place the cases in the cupcake baking tray.
2 Fill each case about three-quarters full with wax pellets. Put in the oven for 5 minutes, or until the wax has melted.
3 Remove the baking tray from the oven and add the dried herbs and flowers to the cases. You can theme your fragrance palette based on the atmosphere you wish to create: dried orange and cinnamon for Christmas, or lavender and bay leaves will set the tone for a relaxing night in.
4 Partially submerge a wick into the wax to aid lighting.
5 Leave the firelighters at room temperature to set, then remove from the baking tray and peel off the cases. Store with your kindling or in a jar on your mantelpiece.
7 To use, place one firelighter on some scrunched up paper or a small pile of kindling. Create a pyramid of kindling around the firelighter, light the wick and enjoy the scents.

Burning bright

Whether you are looking for a decorative, traditional fireplace or a cosy and cost-effective stove, these designs create the perfect antidote to cold autumn evenings

RELIGHT THE FIRE

Many homes are gifted with original fireplaces – these can be in use, disused or completely hidden. Whether you are looking to reinstate an existing fireplace or are unsure of its condition, a chimney sweep will give you an overview of the fireplace's health and functionality before advising on the next steps. For those not lucky enough to uncover original surrounds, reclaimed fireplaces – like this one from Arc Reclamation – can deliver an authentic look and feel to this once-essential part of your home. Arc Reclamation also stocks a range of original fireplace tiles – essential if you want to capture that authentic Victorian fireplace charm.

Burning bright

CONTEMPORARY CLASSIC

ABOVE LEFT Gas stoves are praised for their ease of use, controllability and low maintenance, such as this smart Paragon Edge balanced-flue stove, Charlton & Jenrick. It is compatible with both mains gas or LPG and is designed to be installed where a usable chimney is unavailable. While gas is non-renewable and does release small amounts of carbon dioxide when used, 'modern high-efficiency gas stoves provide instant heat, and balanced-flue gas fires are typically up to 91 per cent efficient,' explains Emma Sheekey, marketing communications manager at Charlton & Jenrick. 'Economically, they are also more cost-effective. Running a gas fire or stove typically costs around 88p per hour. In contrast, woodburning stoves, while variable, can cost around £2.10 per hour, factoring in fuel prices.'

HEARTH AND HOME

ABOVE RIGHT A fire basket, also known as a grate, creates a simple focal point in a classic fireplace setting. Raised sides keep the fuel in place and the grill-like construction allows air to flow through and ash to fall below. 'When choosing a fire basket, think about the fuel you plan to use,' says Simon Bower, technical director at fireplace specialists Percy Doughty. 'Coal burns at a higher temperature than wood, so requires a durable cast-iron fire basket, while wood is compatible with more affordable steel.' Shown here is a basket from the Gallery Valencia/Seville range. 'When burning wood or coal, a fire basket with a black finish is advisable as polished finishes can tarnish quickly,' Simon adds.

ELECTRIC DREAMS

LEFT Bringing heat at the flick of a switch, electric stoves are a good option, especially if you don't have a chimney. Historically, electric stoves were criticised for their unrealistic flames, however, modern designs have become increasingly true to life. Some models, such as this Huntingdon 30 electric stove by Stovax, are nearly indistinguishable from woodburners. According to Stovax, the electric stove costs 34p for an hour of high continuous heating or just 1p for four hours of cosy flame effect.

ELEGANT ADDITION

Choosing the right stove will depend on several factors, including the size of the room and the efficiency of your home's insulation. This can all seem daunting, however specialist Charnwood has an easy online calculator that provides a baseline recommendation based on your room's dimensions. From here, you should contact an experienced installer for a more in-depth survey – including the suitability of your chimney and flue – before purchasing a stove. Shown here is the Cranmore stove in Almond, Charnwood.

Burning bright

ALL ABLAZE

ABOVE LEFT Wood is the most popular fuel for stoves, mostly due to its affordability and the fact that it is carbon neutral. When choosing wood to burn, look for kiln-dried logs or those with less than 25 per cent moisture content to provide a clean burn. 'Green' wood, which has been recently felled, must dry out for at least a year before being burnt. Shown here is the Hunter Herald 5 woodburning slimline double-door Ecodesign stove, from Direct Stoves. Remember that by law, a carbon monoxide alarm must be installed in any room with a solid-fuel appliance.

TRADITIONAL STYLE

ABOVE RIGHT Cast-iron fireplaces are an icon of Victorian interiors; this durable material has wonderful heat-retaining properties, keeping the room cosy and directing heat into the space even when the embers have died. It can be cast into beautifully decorative forms, as seen here in Carron's Victorian combination fireplace, which features traditional motifs, such as baskets of fruit and urn detail, inspired by the era. Cannon's range of fireplaces include Art Nouveau styles, and are compatible with solid fuel – when used with an ash pan – or with gas, which has a coal-effect fire and flames.

GREEN FLAME

LEFT Bioethanol is the latest in sustainable heating. The method involves burning specific alcohol produced from the fermented sugars of the by-products of corn and wheat crops. 'Unlike other fuels, this liquid doesn't create fumes or release smoke, which results in a cleaner heating solution,' explains Jon Butterworth, director at Arada Stoves. 'Bioethanol varies in price, but it's usually around £10 for a one-litre bottle, lasting for between four and five hours. Our stoves, such as the Solution 5 shown here, produce around 2.5kW of heat, which is about the same as an average gas fire, and more than an electric fire.' Unlike gas or woodburning models, bioethanol stoves don't need a flue or ventilation system. They also don't need an electrical outlet. Simply unbox, attached to the wall or floor and use.

Quick-fix refresh

A flick of paint and a flash of colour – spend an hour or two this winter to create these in-the-moment makeovers for your space

Quick-fix refresh

FIREPLACE FEATURE

Opt for chequerboard chic by applying a slim wallpaper border around your fireplace surround. It will create a statement focal point in your living room and can be used to tie together colours and patterns from elsewhere in the space. Not crazy about checks? Choose a stripe or floral design instead, but be sure to echo the motif in two other areas of your scheme for balance.
Ernie wallpaper border in Red, Studio Atkinson. Titan two-seater sofa in Festival Cream/Natural Mix, Sofology

PAINTED FURNITURE

Add a shot of uplifting colour to a room by painting a piece of furniture in a smile-inducing shade. Start by removing any hardware, doors and drawers. If the piece is already painted, rub it down with coarse sandpaper to remove the previous colour, then wipe away any dust. Wash unpainted furniture with sugar soap then sand lightly and wipe clean. Ensure a smooth finish by applying a coat of primer first, then follow with a layer of your chosen paint colour. Allow to dry, then apply a second coat to finish.
For a similar paint colour, try Blooth Pink modern eggshell, Farrow & Ball. Titan wall tiles in Forest; Cuban White Star floor tiles, all CTD Tiles

PILLOW HEADBOARD

This simple idea will perk up a plain bed base – ideal for a guest room. Using a pencil, mark the wall where you'd like each pillow to hang. Next, measure four lengths of slim leather strap around 150cm (5') each and attach in place on the wall using metal tacks. You want to make sure the loops you make can snugly hold your pillows so they don't fall out easily, but still keep their shape. Slide your pillows into the loops and make sure they are supported evenly. Mix up colours and patterns by swapping plain linen covers for something a little bolder.
Natural leather 16mm wide, Leather World Store at Etsy. Linen pillowcases in Natural, The Conran Shop

COLOUR HIGHLIGHTS

This blink-and-you-miss-it stripe, like a slick of coloured eye liner, adds style to an interior door. When it comes to applying a strong colour like this – whether it's a simple stripe on woodwork or a circle to create a background for a wall light – it's important to mark off the area cleanly with decorator's tape. Press the tape edges down firmly, then apply the paint sparingly to avoid drips, even if this means doing two coats. Remove the tape at a 45-degree angle while the paint is still wet for a clean finish.
Door edge in Coral Gables in Regal Select Interior Matte, Benjamin Moore

Homespun Highlands

Bring heartwarming comfort to winter interiors with wool blankets, tactile quilts and handmade pieces inspired by Scottish bothies and rural retreats

Homespun Highlands

Is there anything more appealing than a cosy chair and the expectation of a fire to toast the toes? Warm wintertime floorboards with a thick felted rug

HOMELY NOOK
The bench is antique. For similar, try Urban Chic storage bench, A Place for Everything. Wycombe dining chair, Neptune, is similar. Cushions, from a selection at Tori Murphy, GP&J Baker, Molly Mahon and Rowen & Wren. Sheepskin rug, Toast. Rug, from a selection, French Connection

HEARTHSIDE RETREAT
Bespoke armchair with checked fabric cover, to order, I Gigi. Cornstooks wallpaper in Cloud, Blithfield. For a galvanised fireside bucket, try East2Eden. Abercrombie lamp, Jim Lawrence. Similar cushion, Woodland Fable, John Lewis & Partners. Jannu Radhi rug, Stitch by Stitch

Celebrate the crafted and the reclaimed; pieces that reveal the hands of the maker and the marks of time. We treasure items when we feel their emotional connection

RECLAIM THE PAST
Find reclaimed tiles at Bert & May. Armitage Shanks heavy-duty Belfast sink, Heat & Plumb, is similar

RUSTIC GATHERING
Longworth raw-oak dining chairs, Garden Trading. Coltishall copper verdigris light, Vintage Electrical, is similar. Bowls, from a selection at Leach Pottery, David Mellor and Maud & Mabel

Homespun Highlands

Delightfully patterned throws not only provide layers for chilly evenings, but are perfect for introducing a softer, homespun feel to country interiors

SLEEPING SNUG
Cabin bed built from reclaimed wood, Lassco. Reclaimed wood stool, from a selection, Ines Cole. Kick light in Antique Verdigris, Jamb. Bedlinen, from a selection at Volga Linen and Caravane. Blanket, Caravane. Quilt, from a selection, Stitch by Stitch

IN THE WEAVE
Blankets, from a selection at Damson & Slate, Larusi, The Future Kept, Rowen & Wren, Selvedge, Liberty and Caravane

Haddon cabinets in Mallard Green, Kitchen Makers

Boot room

These simple design ingredients are all you need to create a practical dedicated space for your shoes and outdoor gear

Boot room

PRACTICAL FLOORING
ABOVE LEFT From muddy shoes to rain-soaked coats, boot rooms are a high-traffic area so flooring needs to be a practical choice. Terracotta tiles can be sealed to ensure they stay looking their best. Opt for a herringbone laying pattern for an on-trend modern country vibe.
Marlborough terracotta brick, Artisans of Devizes

PEG RAIL
ABOVE RIGHT A Shaker-style peg rail isn't just handy for hanging coats, bags and umbrellas but also adds a decorative element when used along the length of the entire wall. Finish the look with a rattan shoe storage bench – also the ideal place to sit down to pull off those wellies.
Try Shaker oak coat rack in light grey, John Lewis & Partners

BOOT RACK
RIGHT Freestanding racks which allow you to store wellies upside down mean they will dry more quickly and will keep any wet mud off for floors too – simply move the rack closer to a radiator after particularly wet walks to ensure they're dry and ready for their next outing.
Two pair metal boot rack, Cox & Cox

Winter Home 87

PET AREA
ABOVE LEFT Open shelving keeps pet essentials close to hand on your way in or out from a walk. Work in space for leads, food, treats and even a dog bed, which can be tucked out of sight with a curtain.
Aldsworth bootroom unit; Melcombe bottle shelf in beech, both Garden Trading

WOOD PANELLING
ABOVE RIGHT Classic tongue-and-groove panelling will create a relaxed welcome and protects walls from scuffs. Finish with a coat of washable satin or eggshell paint for extra practicality and paint any other furniture in the same shade for a coordinated result.
Satin paint in Cambrian Blue, Annie Sloan

BUILT-IN BENCH
LEFT Going bespoke with made-to-measure furniture makes the most of every inch of space, and provides dedicated places for even awkwardly shaped items like sports equipment and umbrellas. A lift-up storage bench is the perfect place to hide away boots and wellies.
Cotswold ball cabinet knob, Armac Martin

Rustic glow

YOU WILL NEED
- Mini terracotta pots
- Paintbrush
- Acrylic paint – one light shade and one darker
- Small flexible stencil
- Masking tape
- Stencil brush
- PVA glue
- Ribbon or rickrack
- Plasticine
- Heather
- Pillar candle
- Pencil
- Sand

Banish the darker nights with these simple yet atmospheric potted candle holders

Create a glowing display with these rustic-looking candle holders. Group them together on an industrial-style wall shelf surrounded by foraged finds.

1. Paint the plant pots in the lighter shade of paint. They may need two coats with drying time in between. You can add a small amount of sand to the paint for added texture. Leave the pots overnight to dry fully.
2. Once dry, use masking tape to attach the stencil to the pot. Apply the darker colour paint to the stencil using the stencil brush in a stippling motion for a mottled effect. Alternatively, try painting the pot in a darker shade and stencilling in the lighter one.
3. When completely dry, remove the stencil and seal the pot with a dedicated paint sealant or with a 1:10 mix of PVA glue and water.
4. Glue ribbon or rickrack around the rim of the pot, followed by beaded wire.
5. Cover the hole in the bottom of the pot with some plasticine. You can use this to hold the pillar candle in place. Then fill around the candle with sand.
6. Push a few stems of heather into the sand to decorate, but be sure to keep foliage well clear of the candle's flame.

Pull up your boots

Keep your home organised during the festive chaos by making sure that wet coats and muddy shoes have a home in a practical but also pretty space

PAINTERLY THOUGHTS
Treat functional spaces with the same creativity as other parts of the home – if anything, you can be more experimental as they are not front-facing rooms. With new paint technology, your creative ideas won't be restricted by the need for gloss finishes and darker hues. For example, Little Greene's Intelligent range – available in matt, satin, eggshell and gloss – doesn't require any priming and every finish can resist stains and take knocks, essential in a boot room. For similar paint colours to those shown try Little Greene's Bronze Red and Mushroom, with its Livid on the built-in cuboards. Complete the space with rustic-style wooden furniture, like this Chedworth tall welly locker, from Garden Trading.

FEATURE HOLLY REANEY

PERFECT FIT
When designing a boot room, start by making a list of everything you need from the space – this will guarantee that the room works seamlessly. 'Fitted furniture is an efficient way to optimise space, especially if the bespoke design has been created to fit the exact contours of your room,' explains Rachal Hutcheson, national retail manager at Sharps. 'A beautifully fitted boot room or storage bench is a long-term investment that very often adds value to your home.' Make the most of every inch by opting for multipurpose cabinetry: topping solid floor-level cupboards with a plush seat pad transforms it into a comfortable bench while hiding tiered shoe racks behind wardrobe doors will provide plenty of space for awkwardly shaped footwear. Sharps Shaker boot room in Willow Green.

NATURAL BEAUTY
Botanical prints are the natural choice for boot rooms, providing the perfect link between outdoors and in, creating a practical yet beautiful space. Opting for a design that focuses on foliage rather than flowers creates a more timeless look that will shine whatever the season. Interior designer Whittney Parkinson brought this space to life by dressing walls with Morris & Co's Arbutus wallpaper. This intricate print has been reworked from an archive design by Kathleen Kersey, and refreshed by the Woad/Russet colourway. Using the dusky blue hue of the leaves to define the colours of the woodwork and bench allows the red berries to really pop while bringing out the warmth of the brick tiles and wooden furniture.

Pull up your boots

A TALL ORDER
If a dedicated boot room is not a possibility in your home, you still need somewhere to house your outdoor wear; otherwise, you will quickly find coats hanging off the banisters and piles of shoes cluttering the hallway – ruining the warm welcome to your home. A small freestanding wardrobe cupboard provides plentiful storage, meaning coats and shoes can be shut away and out of sight. Opt for a design like the Cotswold Company's single wardrobe in Chester Dove Grey, which features an oak rail, ideal for letting coats air and dry, as well as a versatile deep drawer for bulky boots. Make the most of the wardrobe's height by adding a few baskets on the base, providing easy-access storage for everyday shoes or bags; store occasional hats in a basket on the top.

TOP TO BOTTOM
Durable flooring is key for a boot room. Carrying the look of natural stone but with improved durability, stone-look porcelain tiles – such as Mandarin Stone's Lincoln sand matt stone effect porcelain tiles – are easy to clean and highly resistant to scratches and stains. They are also compatible with underfloor heating, which can be a valuable addition to a boot room, helping to dry out damp coats and shoes after a winter walk. Drying coats is easier with individual hooks and this is an easy weekend project. Aim to hang hooks around 150cm high and leave a gap of 10 to 15cm between each hook. Hanging hooks on a batten, rather than just into the wall, gives a more finished look and will help it manage the load.

DRESSED TO IMPRESS
Before guests arrive give the boot room the festive treatment. Adding layers of cushions to benches will instantly soften the colder edges of the room, while also providing a warm welcome. You can then add winter decor to bring seasonal character. Festive touches should not reduce the space's usability as the boot room will be in high demand throughout winter, but twinkling lights, solar-powered lanterns, mini Christmas trees and a hanging wreath will provide a magical touch of Christmas. Make the most of dead space by placing baskets under seating areas, in the base of cupboards or above shelves – not only are they practical but they disguise clutter, too. For similar cushions try The White Company.

PANEL SHOW
Adding panelling not only pulls the whole space together but it also helps protect walls from inevitable scuffs and scrapes – especially when painted with a durable finish. If you have unsightly pipework or electrics, these can be boxed in and hidden for a more finished look. Use the building opportunity to also incorporate practical storage with a chest-style bench and a few hooks. In this room, a small open worktop has also been added, providing an out-of-the-way spot for the dog's bed and pet meal-prep space. Matching the fabric on the dog's cushion with the bench pad provides the perfect finishing touch.

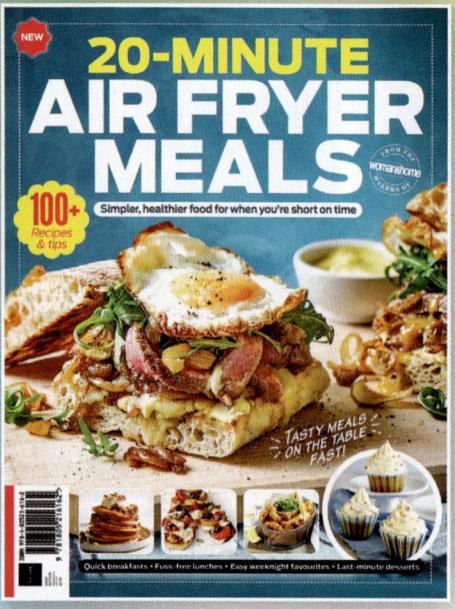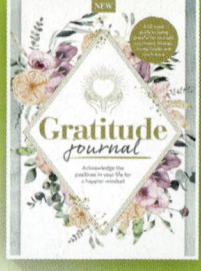

INSPIRING READS FOR A HAPPIER YOU

From travel and food to mindfulness and fitness, discover motivational books to enrich and enhance your life

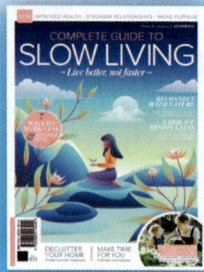

Follow us on Instagram @futurebookazines

FUTURE

www.magazinesdirect.com/lifestyle
Magazines, back issues & bookazines.

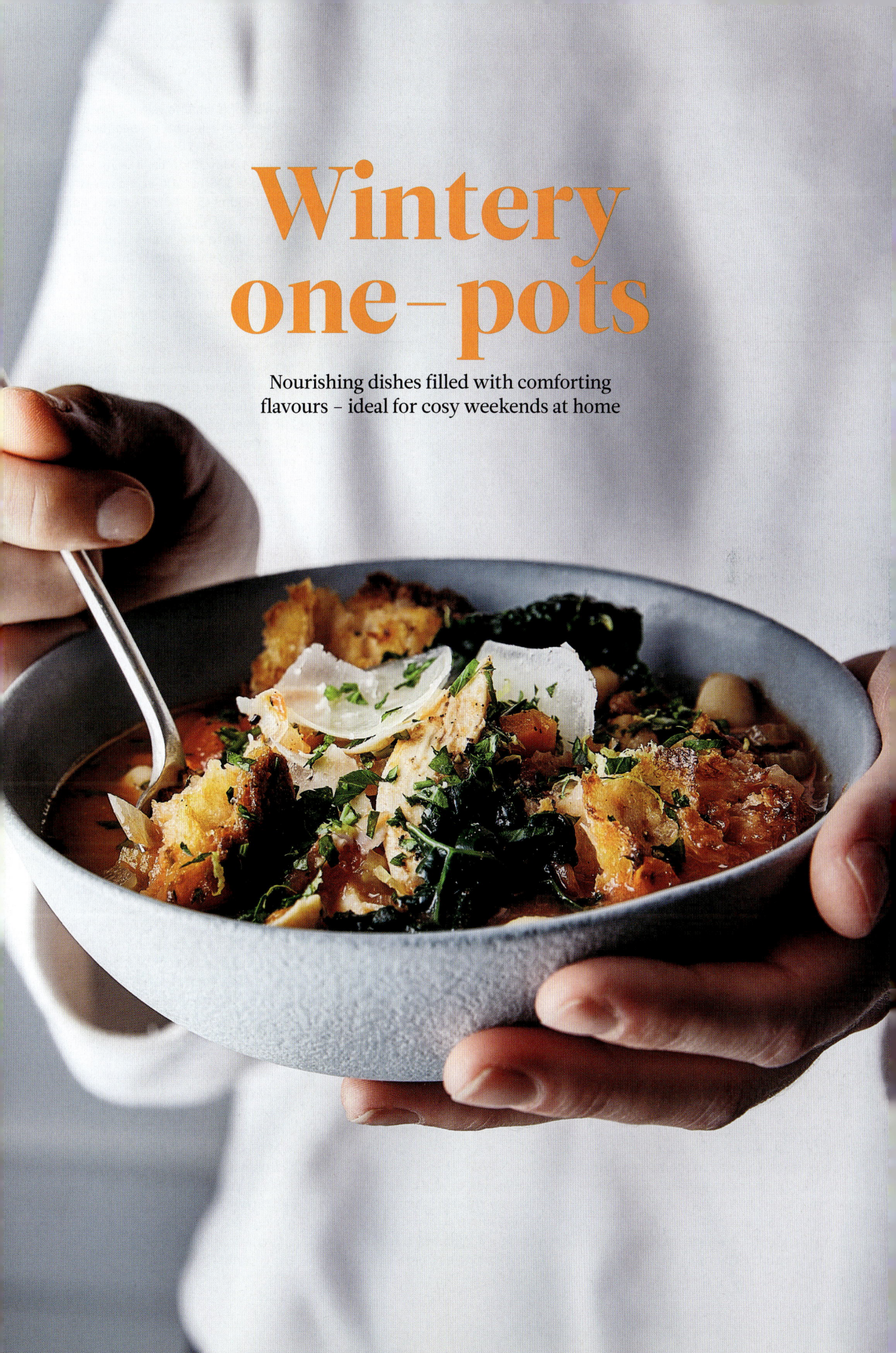

Wintery one-pots

Nourishing dishes filled with comforting flavours – ideal for cosy weekends at home

CHICKEN RIBOLLITA

SERVES 6

We've added chicken to this hearty Tuscan soup to make a filling weekend lunch with bags of flavour.

YOU WILL NEED

- 3tbsp olive oil ● 5 sprigs rosemary, plus extra to garnish ● 1 onion, finely diced ● 1 large carrot, scrubbed clean then finely diced ● 2 sticks celery, finely diced ● 2 garlic cloves, crushed ● 2 x 400g (14oz) tins plum tomatoes ● 400g (14oz) tin cannellini beans in water ● 500ml (1 pint) chicken stock ● 150g (5¼oz) cavolo nero, thick stalks removed and shredded ● 200g (7oz) cooked chicken, chopped or shredded ● 250g (8¾oz) stale bread, preferably sourdough, torn into chunks

TO SERVE

● Parmesan ● Zest 1 lemon ● 2tbsp parsley, chopped

1. Heat the oil in a large casserole dish. Add the rosemary and let it sizzle in the hot oil for 5 mins, then remove the sprigs and discard them.
2. Reduce the heat and add the onion, carrot and celery, and season. Cover and gently fry in the rosemary-infused oil, stirring occasionally for 15 mins, until softened. Add the garlic and cook for 5 mins more.
3. Stir in the tomatoes and half the beans. Crush with the back of a spoon before adding the rest of the beans along with the liquid from the tin.
4. Add the stock and bring to a boil. Season to taste then mix in the cavolo nero and chicken, cover and simmer for 10 mins.
5. Grill the bread for 4 mins. Off the heat, stir the bread into the soup and let it sit for 5 mins before serving with Parmesan, lemon zest and parsley.

BEEF CURRY WITH COCONUT CHUTNEY

SERVES 8-10

Rich and meaty, this easy, make-ahead number will free you from the stove, and it's a great one for the slow cooker.

YOU WILL NEED

● 1tbsp peanut or vegetable oil ● 1.5kg (3¼lb) beef cheek or shin, cut into 6cm (2¼") pieces ● 1 cinnamon stick ● 3 star anise ● 4 cardamom pods, bashed ● 1 stick lemongrass, pressed with the flat side of a knife to release flavour ● 4 fresh lime leaves, bashed (or 8 dried) ● 400ml (13½fl oz) coconut cream (160ml (5½fl oz) if using a slow cooker) ● 300ml (10fl oz) rich beef stock (200ml (6¾fl oz) if using a slow cooker) ● 100g (3½oz) crunchy peanut butter ● 2tbsp dark brown sugar ● 2tbsp tamarind paste ● 2tbsp ketjap manis (or use soy and a little more sugar) ● 2tbsp fish sauce ● 500g (1lb) potatoes, peeled, cut into 5cm (2") pieces

FOR THE CURRY PASTE

● 2 banana shallots, roughly chopped ● 5 garlic cloves, bashed ● 2 red chillies, roughly chopped, plus extra cut into fine strips, to serve ● 5cm (2") piece fresh ginger, finely chopped, plus extra cut into fine strips, to serve ● Juice 2 limes ● 1tbsp lemongrass paste ● 1tbsp ground cumin ● 1tsp ground nutmeg ● ½tsp ground cloves

TO SERVE

● Roti or rice ● Crispy fried shallots ● Roasted peanuts ● Coriander leaves ● Lime wedges ● Coconut chutney

1. Put the curry paste ingredients into a small food processor and whizz until finely chopped.
2. Heat the oil in a large, heavy-based saucepan over a medium-high heat. Season the beef with salt and cook in batches until well browned all over. Set aside on a plate or add to the slow cooker. Add the whole spices, lemongrass and lime leaves, and cook for 2 mins until fragrant.
3. Add the curry paste to the pan and cook, stirring for 2 mins, until darkened, then return the beef to the pan and add the remaining ingredients and some seasoning. Bring to the boil, then reduce the heat to low. Cover and simmer for 2½-3 hrs, until the beef is tender, adding the potato for the last hour. If using a slow cooker, cook on high for 4 hrs, adding the potatoes for the final hour.
4. Taste the sauce and adjust the seasoning with more fish sauce, sugar or lime juice as liked.
5. Meanwhile, for the chutney *(see p97)*, whizz all the ingredients together in a food processor until finely chopped. Season with salt, then set aside.
6. Serve the curry with roti or rice, and top with crispy fried shallots, roasted peanuts, sliced chilli and ginger, coriander leaves, lime wedges and coconut chutney.

Wintery one-pots

COOK'S TIP

Coconut chutney: In a food processor, whizz 100g (3½oz) fresh coconut; 1 green chilli, chopped (remove the seeds for less heat); 2cm (¾") piece ginger, grated; handful coriander leaves; and zest and juice 1 lime

Wintery one-pots

SALMON MAC 'N' CHEESE WITH KIMCHI

SERVES 6

Kimchi adds a punch to creamy, cheesy pasta with smoky salmon – you could swap it for sauerkraut or add cornichons.

YOU WILL NEED
- 250g (8¾oz) macaroni
- 50g (1¾oz) butter
- 3tbsp plain flour
- 500ml (1 pint) whole milk, warmed
- 300g (10½oz) cheese (mix Cheddar, Gruyère and whatever needs using up), grated
- Grating fresh nutmeg
- 200g (7oz) kimchi
- 2 hot smoked salmon fillets, flaked
- 3tbsp panko breadcrumbs
- Chives, chopped (optional)

1. Heat the oven to 220°C/425°F/Gas Mark 7. Boil the macaroni in a pan of salted water for 2 mins less than the pack instructions; drain.
2. Melt the butter in a large pan, then stir in the flour and season. Cook for a few mins, then slowly whisk in the milk until smooth and cook, stirring, until thickened. Stir in most of the cheese until melted and season with nutmeg.
3. Add the drained pasta to the cheese sauce with the kimchi and salmon. Mix to combine, then decant into a large ovenproof dish.
4. Scatter with the remaining cheese and breadcrumbs. Bake for 15-20 mins, until golden and bubbling. Serve with chives and extra kimchi.

SPICED LENTIL AND LAMB SHEPHERD'S PIE

SERVES 6

A richly spiced sauce and silky garlic mash take this a step up from the traditional version, but with all the same comforting texture.

YOU WILL NEED
- 2tbsp olive oil
- 500g (1lb) minced lamb
- 1 large onion, finely chopped
- 3 garlic cloves, crushed
- 2tsp cumin seeds
- 1tsp ground allspice
- 3tbsp tomato puree
- 2-3tbsp harissa paste
- 200ml (6¾fl oz) white wine
- 100g (3½oz) dried apricots, quartered
- 100g (3½oz) dried green lentils, rinsed
- 600ml (1¼ pint) lamb or chicken stock
- Zest 1 lemon
- 100g (3½oz) pitted green olives, halved

FOR THE TOPPING
- 800g (1¾lb) Maris Piper potatoes, peeled and cut into even-sized pieces
- 200ml (6¾fl oz) milk
- 1tbsp salted butter
- 3 garlic cloves

1. Heat the oil in a large, lidded casserole or saucepan, then add the lamb and fry until browned on all sides. Set aside.
2. Add the onion to the pan then cook for 5 mins until softened. Add the garlic, spices, tomato puree and harissa. Cook for 2-3 mins until the paste starts to darken, then stir in the wine. Bubble for 5 mins then return the lamb to the pan along with the apricots, lentils, stock, lemon zest, olives and seasoning.
3. Bring to a boil, then reduce the heat to low and simmer, covered, for 30 mins, until the lentils are tender. Transfer to a high-sided baking dish.
4. Heat the oven to 200°C/400°F/Gas Mark 6 and prepare the topping.
5. Put the potatoes into a pan of cold water, bring to a boil and cook for 20 mins or until tender. Meanwhile, warm the milk until steaming with the butter and garlic; leave to infuse as the potatoes cook, then remove the garlic.
6. Drain and mash the potatoes, then fold in the milk mixture. Spoon the mash over the lamb mixture, then bake for 30 mins until the top of the pie is golden brown and bubbling.

Cosy puddings

A lighter take on some of your favourite desserts

Cosy puddings

ST CLEMENT'S PUDDING

SERVES 6

This dish is based on a lemon self-saucing pudding, where a soufflé-like sponge tops a lovely creamy sauce.

YOU WILL NEED
- 1 lemon ● 75ml (2¾oz) freshly squeezed clementine juice ● 30g (1oz) butter, melted ● 3 medium free-range eggs, separated ● 200g (7oz) caster sugar ● 50g (1¾oz) plain flour ● 1tsp baking powder ● 250ml (8½fl oz) milk

TO SERVE
- Pouring cream

1. Heat the oven to 180°C/350°F/Gas Mark 4 and boil a kettle of water. Grate the lemon zest and squeeze the juice into a measuring jug with the zest. Make the liquid up to 100ml (3½fl oz) with clementine juice.
2. Combine the butter, yolks and sugar in a large bowl and beat until smooth. Sift in the flour and baking powder until combined. Very gradually beat in the milk, a little at a time, and then the citrus juice to form a thin batter.
3. Whisk the egg whites in a separate bowl until firm but not overly stiff. Fold through the batter until evenly incorporated.
4. Pour into a lightly greased 1ltr baking dish and place the dish in a roasting tin. Pour in enough boiling water to come halfway up the sides of the dish. Transfer to the oven and bake for 30-40 mins, until the sponge topping is golden brown. Dust with icing sugar and serve with cream.

PLUM AND CINNAMON CRISP

SERVES 6

A crisp is similar to a crumble, but the topping is less stodgy and more crumbly, perfect for this time of year.

YOU WILL NEED
- 350g (12¼oz) ripe plums, halved and destoned ● 350g (12¼oz) mixed frozen berries, thawed ● 50g (1¾oz) soft brown sugar ● 125g (4½oz) rolled oats ● 30g (1oz) ground almonds ● 50g (1¾oz) pecan nuts, chopped ● 1tsp ground cinnamon ● 50g (1¾oz) butter, melted ● 3tbsp maple syrup

TO SERVE
- Soured cream or Greek yogurt

1. Heat the oven to 200°C/400°F/Gas Mark 6. Put the plums in a bowl with the thawed berries and sugar, and stir well to combine. Transfer to a large ovenproof baking dish.
2. For the topping, put the oats, almonds, pecans and cinnamon in a bowl. Add the melted butter and maple syrup, and stir to combine. Scatter the topping over the fruit, so that it lightly covers it but with some of the fruit still showing through.
3. Transfer to the oven and bake for 25-30 mins until the topping is golden. Serve with soured cream or Greek yogurt.

Winter Home

PEAR AND GINGER STRUDEL

SERVES 8
A modern twist on this classic pastry dessert from Austria and Hungary.

YOU WILL NEED
- 750g (1½lb) ripe pears, peeled and diced
- 50g (1¾oz) fresh white breadcrumbs
- 50g (1¾oz) raisins
- 30g (1oz) soft light brown sugar
- 25g (¾oz) pine nuts, toasted
- 25g (¾oz) crystallised ginger, diced
- 6 sheets filo pastry (ours were 37x28cm (14½x11" each)
- 30g (1oz) unsalted butter, melted
- 150ml (5fl oz) whipping cream
- 1tbsp icing sugar, plus extra to dust
- 1tsp ground cardamom

1. Heat the oven to 200°C/400°F/Gas Mark 6. Line a large baking tray with baking paper.
2. Put the pears in a bowl and add the breadcrumbs, raisins, sugar, pine nuts and chopped ginger. Stir well.
3. Lay a pastry sheet flat on a board and brush with melted butter. Repeat with the remaining pastry to give you 6 buttered layers. Spread the pear mixture over the pastry, leaving a 2cm (¾") border all the way around the edge.
4. Fold the short sides over the filling and brush with butter. Then from one long side, roll up the strudel as tightly and neatly as you can to form a Swiss roll. Make sure the seam of the pastry is on the bottom of the roll.
5. Brush over the remaining melted butter and transfer the strudel to the prepared baking tray. Bake for 30 mins until the pastry is crisp and golden. Remove from the oven, dust all over with icing sugar and leave to cool for 10 mins.
6. Lightly whip the cream, icing sugar and ground cardamom together until firm. Cut the strudel into slices and serve with the cream.

Winter al fresco

Get cosy outdoors with these simple updates and turn your garden into a cocooning entertaining space to celebrate with friends and family

LEADING LIGHTS

Entertaining outdoors at this time of year can be a magical experience, especially as night falls. Layering a mix of atmospheric and functional lighting ensures the celebrations can continue long after the sun goes down. For practicality, electric or battery lights are brighter and longer-lasting, while softer solar-powered designs, like these Solar balloon lanterns from Idyll Home, are perfect for adding a sense of occasion to your gathering. Inspired by hanging Moroccan lanterns, these colourful designs are made of Tyvex, a polyethylene paper that makes them sturdy, water-resistant and long-lasting. Small perforations in the paper create the intricate patterns that glow beautifully when lit up. Simply place the hanging lanterns in full sun during the day to charge, before hanging them where they are needed come nightfall. To optimise the solar panel's charging during winter, place the panels in a south-facing area and wipe the panel with a damp cloth after use.

FEATURE HOLLY REANEY

Winter al fresco

GARDEN SANCTUARY

The name 'summerhouse' suggests this building can only be used during the warmest season; however, with a few alterations, it can also serve as a winter haven – perfect for festive dinner parties. If the building is connected to the mains, an electric stove can be added to heat the space and give it a warming glow – without the complex installation and fire risks of a log burner. Décor also plays a key role. 'Table lamps create lovely pools of light which can be elevated with flickering candles in glass hurricane vases,' says Susie Watson, founder of Susie Watson Designs. 'Sumptuous textures in deep colours add to the warmth – reach for velvets, silks and rustic linens across cushions, tablecloths and napkins.' Embrace the indoor-outdoor atmosphere by adding foraged or faux greenery. 'Our winter flower bunches in hand-blown glass vases add a wonderful splash of rich seasonal colour,' adds Susie.

Luxury Megha linen and velvet tablecloth with tassels, Susie Watson Designs

Winter al fresco

SITTING PRETTY

LEFT Just because it is cold outside, doesn't mean that you can't still utilise your garden furniture. 'The key to making outdoor furniture welcoming in winter is to choose the right set and take good care of it. Season-proof cushions are quick drying so any dew and dampness will disappear long before you and your guests want to sit down,' says Katie McKendrick, brand stylist at Bramblecrest Garden Furniture. A design, like its Chedworth sofa set and table provides plenty of space for everyone to sit, and includes a firepit inset into the table for added warmth. 'When you're not using your set, protect it with a cover and pack away cushions; use a damp sponge and cloth to do a spot clean and dust so all your surfaces are ready to use next time,' advises Katie.

HEART OF GLASS

BELOW Designed to be warm during the coldest months of the year, greenhouses have far more potential than just as a space to overwinter plants. With a table, chairs and a touch of decorative magic, you can create an idyllic spot to dine under the stars. 'Dress the greenhouse as you would your dining room – add artwork and unique accessories for decoration, and include plenty of twinkly lights and candles to create a relaxing ambience,' says Nelly Hall, brand director at Alitex. 'Also consider investing in a greenhouse heater to keep everything cosy and inviting as the temperature drops. This will ensure it stays comfortable as a year-round retreat and you won't have to worry about chilly nights cutting your evening short. Plus, your plants will thank you for the extra warmth, too.'

COOKING UP A STORM

BELOW Traditionally, cooking outdoors is more popular in the summer, but barbecuing in the colder weather can actually help improve the flavour of the food as you cook. 'Winter barbecues bring unique flavour as smoke clings better in cold air, making comfort foods extra delicious,' explains Declan Kingsley-Walsh, managing director at Morsø. However, there are some additional considerations when cooking outdoors at this time of year. 'Cold weather requires more fuel and longer preheating times, so keep extra fuel nearby, and set up in a sheltered but ventilated area. Expect extended cooking times and use a meat thermometer to ensure food is thoroughly cooked. Safety is also essential so clear any snow, use non-slip mats, and add outdoor lighting for darker days. Cover the grill when not in use to protect it from the weather,' adds Declan.

WARMING GLOW

RIGHT If you tend to use a garden building mainly in the summer months, there are a few adjustments you can make to turn it into a useable space all year round. As winter arrives, hanging patio heaters can provide a warming glow and many modern designs – such as those from Kettler – are indistinguishable from pendant lights, meaning you don't have to compromise aesthetics for warmth. Cosy up garden seating with sheepskin throws and sumptuous velvet cushions, and add a rug underfoot to create a welcoming atmosphere that rivals indoors. Candlelight will give the space an inviting feel – recycle glass bottles as candle holders, use lanterns to protect candle flames or swap for LED candles instead, especially if young children will be using the space too. Hanging fairylights from wooden beams will also help turn it into a magical winter hideaway.

Winter al fresco

A winter's tale

There's cold comfort to be had in the winter garden as the season's most resilient plants reveal their true beauty in containers, flower beds and borders

A winter's tale

CONTAINERS

Fill your largest containers with seasonal plants, placing pots where they can be seen from indoors on cold days.

1 GAULTHERIA PROCUMBENS
For an instant, stylish look, use white- or red-berrying gaultheria, combined with dwarf conifers. Add pansies and miniature cyclamen for an extra splash of colour.

2 PHORMIUM
This strappy-leaved evergreen comes in fiery colours that create a bold centrepiece in a large pot, edged with winter bedding in contrasting colours.

3 SANTOLINA CHAMAECYPARISSUS
Shimmering silver leaves of cotton lavender add an elegant touch to pots as a foil for hellebore flowers and gaultheria. As an alternative, use Senecio cineraria 'Silver Dust'.

4 WINTER PANSIES
Pansies will flower for more prolonged periods if you can find plants that are well established in their pots ready for planting. Regularly nip off any fading flowerheads as you pass.

5 SKIMMIA JAPONICA
The variety 'Rubella' provides a richly coloured display and is a traditional feature plant for winter pots. Combine with pansies, violas and trailing ivy.

STUNNING SEEDHEADS

Both ornamental grasses and perennial seedheads look beautiful covered with frost, so delay cutting until spring.

6 SEA HOLLY
Eryngiums are especially dramatic in winter, when their sculptural dried heads and foliage become coated in a covering of frost that makes them look like spiky snowflakes.

7 MISCANTHUS SINENSIS
As with many ornamental grasses, shimmering fountains bring the garden alive with colour and movement from October and remain throughout winter.

8 VERONICASTRUM VIRGINICUM
The garden designers' favourite, this perennial offers tall, pink or white spires in summer and faded spikes add structure in winter.

9 VERBENA BONARIENSIS
This perennial is best cut back to the base in spring to prevent dieback. In the meantime, enjoy the structure of the airy stems when dusted with frost. Mulch roots for winter protection.

WINTER SCENT

Bring life to winter's cold air with scented shrubs. You can also cut flowering stems to perfume your home.

10 DAPHNE BHOLUA
Top of the list for winter scent, waxy pink flowers exude a heady fragrance from November. Plant in a sheltered warm spot on free-draining soil.

11 WINTER HONEYSUCKLE
Good for early foraging bees, position this medium-sized, rounded winter honeysuckle (lonicera) at the back of a border. L. x purpusii will become covered in highly fragrant small tubular flowers.

12 WINTERSWEET
Chimonanthus praecox (wintersweet) couldn't be better named thanks to its intense, sweet scent; the stems of established plants can be cut to bring indoors. In the garden, grow against a warm wall.

13 ABELIOPHYLLUM DISTICHUM
Related to forsythia, this deciduous shrub produces fragrant white or pale pink flowers in February and needs a sheltered, warm spot to thrive.

14 VIBURNUM X BODNANTENSE
If you only have room for one winter scented shrub then make it the upright-growing variety 'Dawn'. The scented white flowers that appear in October are flushed pink; by spring these are more intensely pink.

15 WITCH HAZEL
Hamamelis bears the showiest of flowers in spidery form from late January. H. x intermedia 'Pallida' has a citrus scent and is a reliable choice with good autumn colour. Prefers sun.

WINTER FLOWERS

Plants become noticeable in winter, when frost highlights their form. Choose a sheltered spot for good flowering.

16 CLEMATIS 'ADVENT BELLS'
A vigorous evergreen climber with delightful, nodding bell-shaped creamy flowers with pinky splashes. Perfect planted to climb up a sheltered wall or fence.

17 WINTER JASMINE
If there's one wall shrub you can rely on to flower well, it's this. Bare stems become smothered in unscented yellow flowers, in flushes, from winter to spring.

18 MAHONIA
A stately evergreen for shade, take your pick from 'Winter Sun', with large scented winter blooms; 'Apollo', ideal as ground cover and spring flowers; and 'Soft Caress' (shown), with autumn blooms and good foliage.

19 CAMELLIA 'YULETIDE'
At its peak from November to January, this camellia is aptly named for the festive period. In a smaller garden, grow in a large container of ericaceous compost.

20 ALGERIAN IRIS
Beautiful, lavender-blue flowers with intricate markings appear from December to February above clumps of narrow, strappy leaves. Best in full sun.

21 SNOWDROP
Subtle yet always welcome, delicate snowdrops flower from November, depending on the variety. Galanthus elwesii is one of the earliest or G. 'Atkinsii' (shown) has large outer petals. Plant 'in the green' in February.

A winter's tale

STEMS AND BARK

The winter garden reveals the colours of bark and stems. For bright stems, cut back willows and dogwoods in spring.

22 CORKSCREW HAZEL
An interesting shrub with contortions that form silhouettes in all weathers. Prune Corylus avellana 'Contorta' to keep it manageable.

23 TIBETAN CHERRY
Prunus serrula is a perfect tree for a small garden, its glossy mahogany trunk with peeling bark gleams in winter sunshine.

24 HIMALAYAN BIRCH
The most striking birch for its ghostly white stems, Betula utilis subsp. jacquemontii is often planted in groups or makes an eye-catching feature as a multi-stemmed specimen. Pair with the bright orange-red stems of dogwood, Cornus sanguinea 'Anny's Winter Orange'.

25 SCARLET WILLOW
Stunning Salix alba var. vitellina 'Britzensis' shows off pencil-thick, orange-scarlet stems all winter. Prefers moist soil and full sun.

I spy... in my winter garden

Doctor Sarah Spinney reveals what to look out for

IN THE UK...

Grey squirrel
Grey squirrels can often be seen scurrying around the lawn in winter, foraging for the nuts and acorns they stored during the more bountiful autumn months. Squirrels have also been known to create false caches in order to deter any food thieves.

Redwing
Step outside on a cold, clear night and you may be lucky enough to hear the distinctive 'tsee' call of these winter migrants. By day, flocks of these thrushes can be seen feasting on berry-producing shrubs such as hawthorn. Chopped apple will also entice them in.

Common frog
You might not think that many creatures could survive in the icy depths of your garden pond, but frogs are remarkably resilient creatures. During very cold weather, frogs sink to the bottom of the pond where the frost cannot reach them.

Badger
The badger is becoming an increasingly common visitor to our gardens, even in urban areas. If you spot badgers in your garden, help them through the cold weather by leaving out grapes, mealworms, or even peanut butter sandwiches! Long winter nights increase your chances of seeing these largely nocturnal creatures.

Long-tailed tit
At this time of year, long-tailed tits form small flocks of around 20 individuals. They are easily recognisable with their distinctive plumage, noisy disposition and, of course, their very long tail! To maintain their body temperature during cold winter nights these tiny birds huddle together in dense hedges.

ACROSS THE POND...

Red fox
As the temperature drops these resourceful creatures may pay more regular visits to your garden in search of an easy meal. Foxes breed during the winter so that their cubs are born in spring when food is abundant. Listen out at night for the eerie high-pitched bark of the vixen.

Dark-eyed junco
These small, hardy birds spend their summers in northern coniferous forests. But in winter they are widespread in backyards across the US, often hopping about at the base of your bird feeder. Their colouring varies depending on where you live, so be sure to look up your local junco.

Cedar waxwing
These striking birds are regular backyard visitors to most states during winter. Planting fruit-bearing trees and shrubs such as juniper, hawthorn and winterberry is the best way to attract them to your home. Hundreds of waxwings may flock together to feast once they find a good spot.

Raccoon
During very cold weather, raccoons enter a state of semi-hibernation known as torpor. Their body temperature lowers and their blood sugar levels drop, so they can sleep in their dens for weeks. During mild spells, they are a common sight in gardens, urgently scavenging for food.

White-tailed deer
Although not always the most welcome of backyard visitors, remember that winter is a tough season for deer. Their long legs and pointed hooves are not designed for walking on snow, making your recently ploughed driveway a very appealing place to conserve some valuable energy!

YOU WILL NEED
- Mini silicone ring cake or bundt tin(s)
- 200g (7oz) lard
- 100g (3½oz) bird feed
- Twine
- Wooden spoon
- Microwavable bowl
- Ribbon
- Fir sprigs
- Twigs with berries

Feed the birds

Keep feathered friends well-fed over winter by creating this festive swag with a difference

Once the first frost hits, food becomes scarce for garden birds, so help to support them by growing plants rich in berries and putting out dedicated feeders. At this time of year, foods high in fat like this feeder are especially valuable, helping our winged visitors to bulk up and survive the cold weather.

1. Place the lard in a microwavable dish and melt in the microwave in 15-second blasts, stirring between each, until the lard has melted fully.
2. Mix in the bird feed. Opt for a mix of different types and sizes of feed to attract a variety birds to your garden. Mealworms, sunflower seeds and millet are popular with most species. Then fill the silicone cake tin or tins with the mixture and place in the freezer to set.
3. Gather the fir sprigs in a bouquet and tie them together with twine. Add the twigs and berries, tying them in place. The berries will add colour to the display and provide additional food for the birds.
4. After 24 hours, remove the feeders from the freezer and turn out from the tray. Loop twine through the centre of the feeders and tie them to the bouquet.
5. Hang your swag in the garden, somewhere quiet close to natural shelter such as trees or shrubs.

Freeze frame

Capture the beauty of your garden and the countryside in winter with our expert photography guide

Freeze frame

The garden is transformed in wintertime, when frost will snag hold of decorative ironwork and flower buds, or create a glistening outline of branches and leaves. The effect is all-too transient, frost crystals melting as the winter sun steals up into the sky. That is why so many photographers love to be out early, capturing plants and the landscape in silvery raiment.

Like all artists, professional photographers see the world in sharper focus, and will translate a frosty seedhead or a lawn into a magical, unexpected image. They will often choose scenes that are backlit, shooting into the sunlight against standard practice, or will give more emphasis to an icy detail by deliberately blurring the background and by playing with the depth of field.

To find out how to create images like the ones on these pages by photographer Annaïck Guitteny, we asked some top photographers for starting points. So, wrap up well, get your eye in and seek out strong shapes and silhouettes in your garden and beyond – you may find yourself taking a winter wonderland of frosty moments.

GET READY TO FOCUS
Landscape photographer Adrian Oakes offers practical advice for getting started.
- Dress for standing still. Layers, a hat, gloves, warm boots and two pairs of socks are essential. Batteries do not last as long in cold weather but can be revived by warmth. Keep spares in an inside pocket, and swap them regularly.
- Head out before sunrise. Once the sun appears, you are on borrowed time, although the frost will last a little longer in shady areas.
- Avoid windy conditions. Everything will move and blur if the exposures are longer.
- Keep an eye out for hoarfrost – the needle-like white ice crystals are worth an early start.

LONG-DISTANCE SHOTS
- Look for frost patterns, especially on glass, frozen ponds and puddles, and for low sunlight streaming through frosty trees.
- Consider the quality of light and its direction.
- On an SLR camera, you will require a lens of 200mm or higher for a landscape shot. To zoom in on a detail in the distance, you will need a narrower aperture of f5.6 to f6.3, and for a foreground shot, a wide aperture of f9 to f11.

CLOSE-UP SHOTS
- Use a 105mm macro lens, to close in on the patterns and crystalline textures.
- Backlighting adds impact to frosty leaves. Position your camera to take advantage of early winter sunrise and shoot into the light.
- Frost-covered cobwebs look amazing; spiky leaves and frozen flowers are also striking.
- Try not to breathe on the frosted delicacies.
- Hold an A4 black card behind attractive specimens so they stand out. In poor light, a tripod is essential to achieve extra-sharp photos.
- Bright frost and snow may confuse the camera's metering, making shots look dull. Expose to compensate.
- Use a larger aperture for isolating subjects and to blur the background, and a smaller one for depth of focus. An SLR camera gives control and focus through the optical viewfinder. For shallow depth and to isolate a single object against a blurry background, use an aperture of f2.8 to f4.

SMARTPHONE PHOTOGRAPHY
Take beautiful shots on your smartphone with these tips from expert Royston Matthews.
- Sunrise and sunset often provide warm light that can enhance the beauty of a winter landscape. Backlighting allows for interesting silhouettes. Side lighting will emphasise texture. Light from behind the camera (front lighting) will give the most even light on the subject.
- Instead of shooting just at eye level, explore low and high options to create more interesting images. If your phone has a telephoto lens use this for variety and to isolate sections of the landscape. Avoid using the digital zoom as this will decrease image quality.
- Close-up images are very much enhanced by the choice of background. Look for good colour and contrast combinations between the subject and what's behind.
- Blur the background. Some phones have a portrait mode which will blur the background while keeping the subject in sharp focus – this works especially well on close-ups of flowers and berries. Portrait mode in combination with a telephoto lens can be very effective.
- With all phone photography make sure the lenses are kept clean for best results. If your phone can shoot RAW files then this will allow for the best quality. On days with a lot of light and high contrast, consider using the phone's HDR option to increase the tonal range of the image.

CAPTURING THE MOMENT
Allan Pollok-Morris has these ideas to get great results.
- Be aware of leaving footprints in the frost-covered grass or snow, which will spoil the effect of the photograph.
- Trying a variety of shots of your subject can often give something unexpected, particularly if your camera allows different focus, shutter speeds and apertures.
- White attracts what the human eye goes for, but the camera has a real problem with it. So, if you are using a point-and-shoot camera, shorten your shutter speed – preset it to -1.5 or -2; you will make the picture darker but will capture the detail.

JASON INGRAM ON WHAT TO LOOK FOR.
- Do not cut back seedheads; frosty seedheads are a joy to photograph.
- Look for structure, shape and architectural details, such as gates, fences and statues.
- Get down low, as winter flowers are often small and close to the ground.
- Occasionally take your camera off your tripod – not all shots need to be sharp throughout.

PHOTOGRAPHY COURSES
Jason Ingram offers an online Garden & Landscape Photography Masterclass with Create Academy.
The four-hour course includes 27 lessons and a downloadable workbook; createacademy.com
Dawn 2 Dusk Photography runs landscape photography workshops, from Snowdonia to Scotland; dawn2duskphotography.co.uk
Royston Matthews is a West Sussex-based photographer. As well as his own courses (rjmphotography.com), he teaches at West Dean College of Arts & Conversation; westdean.ac.uk

'The "golden hours" of sunrise and sunset provide warm light that can enhance the beauty of a winter. Backlighting allows for interesting silhouettes, while side lighting will emphasise texture'

Bathing beauty

Embrace the relaxing qualities of lavender with this soap recipe that combines soothing essential oils and dried flower buds

YOU WILL NEED
- 1kg (2¼lb) melt-and-pour soap base, try The Soap Kitchen
- Knife
- Glass bowl
- Saucepan
- Wooden spoon
- Lavender essential oil
- Soap mould of your choice
- Dried lavender flowers
- Spray bottle with isopropyl alcohol (optional)

Believed to have been introduced to Britain by the Romans, lavender has been adored for millennia. Incorporate the powerful herb into your daily routine with this soap recipe to make at home, using an easy melt-and-pour soap base.

1. Cut the soap base into smaller cubes – this will help it to melt evenly. Place the cubes in the glass bowl.
2. Pour boiling water into the base of the saucepan and place the glass bowl on top. Make sure that the bottom of the bowl does not touch the water. Heat the pan on a low heat to melt the soap base, stirring occasionally to ensure it melts evenly – do not allow it to boil. When fully melted, remove from the heat.
3. Add around 15ml (½fl oz) lavender essential oil and stir. You can use less if you want a milder fragrance, but any more may prevent the soap setting.
4. Pour half of the fragranced soap over the mould's base, working quickly so that it doesn't start to set in the bowl. Then sprinkle the dried lavender flowers over the surface. Follow with the rest of the melted soap mixture.
5. If desired, spray the surface with the alcohol to remove any unwanted bubbles. The bubbles won't affect the quality, but they will be visible in the finished soap.
6. Leave the mixture to set overnight.
7. Turn out your soap. If using a large mould, cut your soap into usable slices; on average, 1kg (2¼lb) of soap base should make somewhere between nine and 13 bars.

Warming up

Whether you choose to build your own or buy a ready-made design, enjoy evenings in the garden even as the mercury drops with a cosy firepit

SWITCHED ON
For warmth at the flick of a button, gas firepits offer a simple and smokeless alternative to traditional wood-burning designs. 'With a gas fire pit, you can enjoy the immediate warmth and ambience of a real fire without the trouble of trying to get the fire started,' says Richard Searle, head of product for Kettler. 'Another added benefit is their practicality – they can be effortlessly integrated into tables and covered when not in use.' While gas canisters, such as those used with this design, can be connected on a DIY basis, if using mains gas, always seek professional assistance. Kettler Palma low firepit table in Oyster.

COOKING UP A STORM
TOP LEFT If space is tight, then consider a firepit that can double up as a barbecue. This Outdoor Henley fireplace, from Ivyline, not only features a generous fire pit and has space for storing spare logs, but it also comes with a stainless steel griddle, allowing you to cook alfresco meals above the flames. Crafted from iron with a patinated rust finish, the enclosed design also means you don't have to worry about inclement weather or water gathering in the pit.

PICK YOUR SPOT
LEFT The location of a firepit will be guided by safety and usage. 'There is a strong temptation to build the firepit far away from the house, to make it more of a destination, but I find that a more centrally located pit will get the most use and enjoyment,' says Kryssie Maybay, landscape architect at Kismet Design. For open bowl designs, such as this Foscot fire pit, from Garden Trading, it is also important to note the wind direction and avoid placing seating in the pathway of smoke – a movable fire pit or garden furniture will be ideal in these circumstances. As with any open flame, ensure it is at least 3 metres away from anything flammable – such as trees, decking or furniture.

BURNING UP
BOTTOM LEFT With higher sides, Morsø's cast-iron Jiko firepit, offers a more compact alternative to open bowl designs – ideal for smaller gardens or patios. 'Selecting the right wood to burn is vital for ensuring safety and achieving optimal efficiency. Only use seasoned wood – which has been dried for at least six months – and avoid wood that has been treated, painted and stained, or plywood and MDF, as these can release harmful chemicals which can pose health risks and comprimise the firepit,' says managing director Declan Kingsley-Walsh. 'The size of the logs will also impact efficiency. Smaller, split logs will help maintain optimal airflow and provide a more steady burn.'

CLASSIC STYLE
RIGHT With an instantly recognisable vase-like shape, the tradition of clay chimneas is centuries old. Designed to maximise warmth regardless of the weather, they were originally used in Mexico as a method of cooking and heating. Today, they are more commonly found in gardens but still serve similar purposes. 'Whether you choose a metal or clay design, both add charm and warmth to any alfresco evening,' says Darren Craven, furniture lead at British Garden Centres, which stocks a range of chimnea designs. 'Chimneas also provide widespread heat and can be easily moved to maximise heat distribution. Additionally, their tall design helps to save space so are perfect for even the tiniest of gardens.'

HOME MADE
FAR RIGHT Whether built from stones, bricks or slabs, it is surprisingly straightforward to safely construct your own firepit on a cleared and level patch of ground. Designing and building a firepit is often more cost-effective than purchasing an off-the-shelf model and also gives you the freedom to create a design that seamlessly integrates into your garden or patio area and complements your home's traditional exterior.

Warming up

BUILD YOUR OWN
Design a bespoke firepit and build it yourself with this advice from the experts

When designing a built-in firepit, your main choice is between a raised design, in which bricks form a wall around the flames, or a sunken one, with the firepit constructed below ground in a purpose-built depression. Kryssie Maybay elaborates: 'A sunken firepit will provide more heat around your legs, whereas, with a raised pit, this area is shielded from the heat, which makes raised pits better for families with small children.' Raised designs also tend to be easier to install on a DIY basis.

MATERIAL MATTERS
When building a firepit, ensure that it has a stable base and that the firepit walls are at least 30cm (12") deep and 45cm (18") high. The average firepit can easily exceed 900°C (1652°F) in temperature, so fire-resistant materials are essential. 'Fire bricks, also known as refractory bricks, are an ideal choice for lining a firepit,' advises Neil Thomas, co-owner of Firepit.co.uk. 'Another option is to use natural stone such as granite and limestone which can withstand high temperatures, or consider heat-resistant concrete, as it can be poured and shaped to fit the desired design. Avoid traditional concrete, though, as this can crack under high temperatures.'

SAFETY FIRST
'To reduce the risk, a spark guard or fire screen helps prevent embers from escaping the firepit. Always have a bucket of water or fire extinguisher on hand. It is also very important to never leave a firepit unattended,' adds Neil Thomas.

DRAINAGE
The enemy of fire is water and a waterlogged firepit will be of little use. There are two approaches to managing this. The first is a cover – if water can't get in, there is no need for drainage. Metal covers are preferable but if using a plastic or canvas cover, ensure the fire is completely extinguished and cold before using this. Covering a firepit will also reduce the impact of weathering. Without a cover, you will need to include a drainage system. The experts at Walden Backyards advise to 'install a drainage layer beneath a firepit. If the base is solid, you'll need drainage holes; if the bottom is a grate, you won't need holes. You can use lava rocks, firepit glass or gravel to create a drainage layer about 30cm (12") deep.'

VENTILATION
Good airflow is essential to provide oxygen to promote burning and reduce emissions. Ventilation is easier to incorporate into a raised firepit – simply add a gap between the bricks, opt for fire bricks with air holes, or install a grate or flue pipe. The holes must be on at least two sides.

For a sunken design, ventilation is more complex. 'Depending on depth, a sunken firepit will require a pipe to be fitted. This will typically run from the base and be dug through the ground away from the fire, with a right angle at the end sticking up out of the ground,' says Chris Harrington, founder of Harrington Porter Garden Design.

New Year's resolutions

There's no better time to think about the year ahead than now. Look forward to a fresh start and commit to improving your home and garden, learning new skills, and making a positive impact with these ideas

GROW YOUR GARDENING SKILLS

During lockdown, millions of people found sanctuary in their gardens, resulting in an upsurge in green-fingered pursuits, from growing fruit and veg on the patio to creating new flower beds. Gardening is a vast subject area that takes many years to fully master, but you don't need to be an expert to enjoy it, and often the best way to build your experience and learn what works in your own garden is through trial and error.

A good place to start is to assess your plot and soil type – which areas are mainly in the sun, and which are partially or fully shaded? Do you have heavy clay-based soil, free-draining sandy or chalky soil, or perfect loamy soil? Invest in a soil-testing kit to find out if it is more acidic or alkaline. Answers to these questions will guide you towards choosing 'the right plant for the right place'.

While it's tempting to buy plants from the garden centre simply because you like the look of them, consider not just whether they are right for your garden, but how they will work together in terms of colour, texture and eventual size. Gifted gardeners will plan for there to be something in flower in every season, from winter hellebores and spring bulbs to summer roses and autumn dahlias.

As well as creating an attractive garden, consider growing your own fruit and vegetables. While some need a lot of space, there are a number that can be planted in smaller areas and pots: try runner beans, courgettes, beetroot, tomatoes and berry fruits, plus a few herbs to provide a feast for the senses.

A gardening course is a great way to accelerate your learning and to begin discovering different plants. The RHS website lists regional and online courses, teaching you how to select plants and care for your garden. There are also many less-formal workshops you can attend – try Sarah Raven.

Illustrations Sarah Overs Words Mel Lloyd

New Year's resolutions

TAKE UP A NEW CRAFT

From sewing to ceramics, there is a craft to suit every taste and skill level. You don't need to be especially artistic to have a go, but it's a wonderful way to nurture your creativity and indulge in some valuable 'me time'. This is about enjoying yourself, so it doesn't matter if your early attempts aren't worthy of display. But hopefully, with a bit of practice, you will hone your craft and create something you can feel proud of. If you're already accomplished at one type of craft, then push yourself to try something new this year. If you become really good, you could even turn your hobby into a business, selling your wares locally or on online marketplaces such as Etsy. Here are some crafts to try your hand at:

EMBROIDERY is ideal for novices, as there are a wealth of kits on offer that provide beginner's guides to different stitches. Try your hand at making pictures and cushions, and customising clothes and linens. Hawthorn Handmade sells embroidery kits that come complete with a wooden hoop that can be used to display your finished work.

HAND PRINTING is a fun activity that requires little skill or equipment, but can be used to customise everything from teatowels and cushions to wrapping paper. Indian printing blocks produce stunning results, or you can cut out your own designs from lino or potatoes.

POTTERY is the ideal hobby to embrace your artistic flair, and to create unique pieces for your home. You can complete small projects, such as plant pots and trinket dishes, with air-dry clay such as Sculpd, but for glazed ceramics you'll need access to a kiln. Book onto a course at a local college or craft centre.

BASKETRY is an option for the more practical minded who want to make something they can actually use. It's an ancient craft that employs specialist techniques and tools, so it's a good idea to go on a course – see craftcourses.com. You can also use these skills to make your own willow garden sculptures.

SUPPORT LOCAL HERITAGE

If you have enough free time, then consider helping out a local heritage organisation, property or museum. Not only is it incredibly rewarding to provide much-needed support, but you could learn a huge amount about history, get upclose with artefacts and meet new people.

Contact local venues to see if any are looking for volunteers. The National Trust is usually supported by a huge team, so it's worth checking the types of roles you could do in future. There are many different ways you can help a heritage organisation, including as a room guide, archivist, gardener, or working in the shop. However, Covid prevented many venues from raising money for maintenance work, and continuing inflation have left may museums struggling, so consider that making a donation still might be one of the best ways to support them.

DO YOUR BIT TO HELP WILDLIFE

Providing food and refuge for animals and beneficial insects in your garden is a great way to support local wildlife. Not only is it satisfying to help them to grow in number, but it's lots of fun to spy on birds, bees, butterflies and other minibeasts. There are many declining species in the UK, including hedgehogs, bats, sparrows, song thrushes and stag beetles, while precious pollinators such as bees and hoverflies have significantly decreased in number due to the loss of their natural habitat.

One of the simplest things you can do to help wildlife is to plant more bee-friendly flowers, which will also appeal to other creatures. The Bumblebee Conservation Trust publishes a comprehensive plant list at bumblebeeconservation.org, with an interactive tool to see how your garden currently fares.

There's plenty of other things you can do to help wildlife, too – instead of having a plain fence, create a living boundary full of flowers and berries; leave an area of wild lawn to mimic a meadow; hang feeders for birds with a choice of seed and fat balls; add a pond to attract newts and dragonflies, and provide water for birds; build a bug hotel and a hedgehog house; and put up bat and bird boxes to provide nesting spots.

Get one step closer to nature by volunteering with an organisation in your local area. If there is a community garden or woodland, you could assist with maintenance. You could also help to care for nature reserves and survey protected species. Check **wildlifetrusts.org** for opportunities in your area.

INVEST IN YOUR HOME

Will this be the year that you finally extend the kitchen, replace the bathroom or revamp the hallway? When it comes to setting New Year's resolutions, home-improvement ambitions often feature highly, but it's all too easy to let another year go by without achieving your dreams. Start by making a list of key priorities – either whole rooms or elements such as fitting a stove or repainting the windows – and arrange them in order of importance. Next, decide your budget and how much you realistically have available to spend on the house this year, preferably without taking out loans. Finally, consider work and other commitments, as if you have a busy full-time job or take care of dependents, it will limit DIY and make life stressful if you take on too much. With all this in mind,

New Year's resolutions

BE MORE ECO-FRIENDLY

There are many changes – big and small – that you can make to live more sustainably and minimise your impact on the planet. The good news is that it doesn't always have to be expensive or difficult, so make this the year you reduce your footprint at home, starting with these simple ideas:

UPCYCLING is a brilliant way to create something unique, reduce waste and save money on buying new. You can upcycle everything from large pieces of furniture to small items like trays and picture frames. As long as the item has an appealing shape, it can be transformed into something desirable. Annie Sloan makes fabulous Chalk Paints to help you create your masterpiece.

DRAUGHTS are a common issue in period homes, causing discomfort and heat loss. If your instinct is to turn up the heating, then see where you can reduce gaps – add chimney balloons to open fireplaces, fit secondary glazing to original windows, seal gaps in floorboards and use draught excluders at doorways to keep in warmth.

INSULATION is probably the best thing you can invest in to reduce energy use – and lower bills. The loft is the easiest and cheapest place to add more insulation, starting at a few hundred pounds. Ideally use natural, breathable materials such as sheep's wool.

LED LAMPS have a reputation for being expensive and not performing in the same way as traditional bulbs. However, not only do modern designs create a very natural-feeling light, but they use approximately 85% less energy than standard bulbs, and last ten times as long. You could even save over £200 a year by making the switch.

GARDENS shouldn't be overlooked in your quest to be more eco-friendly. Instead of binning food scraps, add them to a compost heap to create an excellent soil improver; fit a water butt to store rainwater for thirsty plants; and make the switch to natural pest control solutions.

you can begin to price up the work.

If you're planning on moving in the next couple of years, then unless you bought it as an obvious 'project house' with huge potential for extending and renovating, it's best to prioritise those jobs that will add most value with least investment. Keeping on top of general maintenance and repair will reduce the ability for future buyers to negotiate a reduced purchase price, while freshening up the décor will make it more appealing for sale.

If this is your forever home, it's important to take the time to get things right and invest in the best quality materials and furnishings you can afford. Think about the order of works – if you decorate two bedrooms this year, but then decide to overhaul the house's electrics or plumbing next year, then it could affect the work you are doing now. While finishing those jobs ahead of decoration may make you feel like you're further away from your goal, the end result will be better for it.

Winter Home

Future PLC Quay House, The Ambury, Bath, BA1 1UA

Editorial
Group Editor **Philippa Grafton**
Senior Designer **Briony Duguid**
Head of Art & Design **Greg Whitaker**
Editorial Director **Jon White**
Managing Director **Grainne McKenna**

Cover images
Future Content Hub / Dan Duchars

Photography
All copyrights and trademarks are recognised and respected

Advertising
Media packs are available on request
Commercial Director **Clare Dove**

International
Head of Print Licensing **Rachel Shaw**
licensing@futurenet.com
www.futurecontenthub.com

Circulation
Head of Newstrade **Tim Mathers**

Production
Head of Production **Mark Constance**
Production Project Manager **Matthew Eglinton**
Advertising Production Manager **Joanne Crosby**
Digital Editions Controller **Jason Hudson**
Production Managers **Keely Miller, Nola Cokely,
Vivienne Calvert, Fran Twentyman**

Printed in the UK

Distributed by Marketforce – www.marketforce.co.uk
For enquiries, please email: mfcommunications@futurenet.com

GPSR EU RP (for authorities only)
eucomply OÜ Pärnu mnt 139b-14 11317, Tallinn, Estonia
hello@eucompliancepartner.com, +3375690241

The Winter Home First Edition (HOB7613)
© 2025 Future Publishing Limited

We are committed to only using magazine paper which is derived from responsibly managed, certified forestry and chlorine-free manufacture. The paper in this bookazine was sourced and produced from sustainable managed forests, conforming to strict environmental and socioeconomic standards.

All contents © 2025 Future Publishing Limited or published under licence. All rights reserved. No part of this magazine may be used, stored, transmitted or reproduced in any way without the prior written permission of the publisher. Future Publishing Limited (company number 2008885) is registered in England and Wales. Registered office: Quay House, The Ambury, Bath BA1 1UA. All information contained in this publication is for information only and is, as far as we are aware, correct at the time of going to press. Future cannot accept any responsibility for errors or inaccuracies in such information. You are advised to contact manufacturers and retailers directly with regard to the price of products/services referred to in this publication. Apps and websites mentioned in this publication are not under our control. We are not responsible for their contents or any other changes or updates to them. This magazine is fully independent and not affiliated in any way with the companies mentioned herein.

Future plc is a public company quoted on the London Stock Exchange (symbol: FUTR)
www.futureplc.com

Chief Executive Officer **Kevin Li Ying**
Non-Executive Chairman **Richard Huntingford**
Chief Financial Officer **Sharjeel Suleman**

Tel +44 (0)1225 442 244